LESBOMANIA

by Jorjet Harper

LESBOMANIA

Humor, Commentary and New Evidence That We Are Everywhere

Withdrawn

by Jorjet Harper

Illustrations by Joan Hilty

New Victoria Publishers Inc.

Published by New Victoria Publishers Inc., a feminist, literary, and cultural organization, PO Box 27, Norwich, VT 05055-0027.

Cover Art and Illustrations by Joan Hilty

First printing.
Printed on recycled paper

Library of Congress Cataloging-in-Publication Data

Harper, Jorjet, 1947-
  Lesbomania / by Jorjet Harper.
     p.   cm.
  ISBN 0-934678-53-7 : $9.95
  1. Lesbianism--United States. 2. Lesbianism--United States--Humor.
  I. Title.
    HQ75.6.U5H37 1994
    305.48'9664--dc20   94-809
                                                  CIP

1807-104-1432

For Sappho
who knew we would think of her
in a future time

And for Kat
who is very much loved
and remembered

Acknowledgments

Many people have contributed to the creation of this book—some in ways too profound to explain here, some through conversations that sparked a lesbomaniacal train of thought for me, some by taking the time and responsibility to arrange readings and performances of my work, some by offering me a forum for publication, some by letting me know they enjoyed my columns and looked forward to reading them, and some simply by saying or doing something that encouraged me to continue.

Many thanks to Tracy Baim of Lambda Publications in Chicago for her enthusiasm for my work, for providing a welcoming outlet for publication for so many lesbian and gay writers through the years, and for her tireless efforts for lesbian and gay liberation.

Thanks to Marcy J. Hochberg for her thoughtful editing of my original columns, for the gifts (she knows which ones), and for the occasional Hunter Girl nostalgia.

A special thank you to Alix Dobkin, Paula Walowitz, Micki Leventhal, and Lynn Siniscalchi for their help in creating the original "radio news show" version of "The War Between the Butches and the Femmes" series.

Thanks to Jeannie Durkin and Paula Walowitz for their enduring friendship and good advice, and for the standing invitation to watch *Star Trek* on their color TV.

Thanks to Anne Hills, a woman of a calm heart, for many years of friendship and beautiful music, and to Tamlyn Raven Moss for making her mommy glad to be a mommy.

Thanks to Paula Berg for her friendship, wit, humor, incredible energy, wise words, encouragement, and for the *au natural* basketball games in the swimming pool at Southern Fest.

Thanks to Julie Parson for her solid support, advice, and continued friendship through thick and thin, even over long distances.

Thanks to Michèle Bonnarens for her unflagging support of Lesbomania; for talking me into visiting Berlin, the superdykiest city in Europe; and for once telling me that she wants to be like me when she grows up.

Danke schön to Anja Kofbinger, the first woman to attain the degree of Doctor of Lesbonautics, for her hospitality, for her own general intense, original, Berlinische lesbomania, and for coaching me in how to say "portajane" in German (ein por-tah-bluh twa-let-tuh).

Like, Thanks to Micki Leventhal and Con Buckley, for their solstice and equinox parties and scintillating conversations, and to Micki for the spontaneous duet lip-synching to the Shangri-Las' "Leader of the Pack."

Thanks to Dolores Connelly and Leslie Wardlaw for their love, support, encouragement, and for my floor-length parlor curtains.

Grazie to Kathy Sara for all the phone calls and so much more, and to Michelle Coffin for making Kathy happy.

Thanks to Toni Armstrong, Jr. for her unflagging support of my writing, for her unerring devotion to lesbian culture, and for the happy memories of past times shared.

Thanks to Angie Schmidt for her smile, for the visits, the home cooking, the Enya tape, and for taking the air conditioner out of my window.

Thanks to Yvonne Zipter forever, and for the haiku.

Salut et merci to Veronique for laughing at my jokes in that dark lesbian bar in Paris, and for continuing to keep in touch.

Merci beaucoup to Nadine Baumgartner and all those fabulous French lesbians of *Lesbia* Magazine.

Many thanks for various reasons to: Claudia Allen, Karen Anderson, Lillian Anguiano, Carol Anshaw, Terry Baum, Alison Bechdel, Pat Bechdolt, Laurie Benz, Kathie Bergquist, Michal Brody, Linda Bubon, Vicki Byard, Rhonda Casady, Loretta Cattani, Peggy Christiansen, Ann Christophersen, Fred Cohen, Carole Crawford, Michele Crone, Chris Crosby, Susie Day, Alix Dobkin, Tom Donelan, Kris Drewes, Ted Dvoracek, Neil Eddinger, Rose Fennell, Kathy Ford, Nancy Floy, Scott Galiher, Martha Gass, Michele Gautreaux, Val Glaser, Brenda Goldstein, Jewelle Gomez, Vernita Gray, Barbara Grier and Donna McBride, Kim Griffin, Lorraine Harris, Gillian Hanscombe and Suniti Namjoshi, Mary Hauck, Susan Herr, Sue Hill, Sarah Lucia Hoagland, Jerry Howard, Natalie Hutchison, Kris Johnson, Gina Kazan, Fran Kao, Kris Kovick, Marie Kuda, Lola Lai Jong, Annie Lee, Riva Lehrer, Debby Mars, Armistead Maupin, Mother Superior a.k.a. Mary McCauley, Andrew Miller, Cheryl Miller, Miranda of Lesbich Archief Leeuwarden Nederland, Lilian Mohin, Kathy Munzer, Marilyn Mueller, MJ Murphy, Laurie Moses, Achy Obejas, Marilyn O'Leary, Deidre O'Malley, Cliff O'Neill, Pat Parker, Leah Paster, Mary Patten, Julia Penelope, Rachel Pepper, Sarah Pettit, Sandra Pollack and Denise Knight, Nancy Poore, Dawn Popelka, Erica Rand, Ruthann Robson, Joy Rosenblatt, Itala Rutter (wherever you may be), Louise Schaefer, Michaelangelo Signorile, Ruth Simkin, Dev Singh, Lynn Siniscalchi, Victoria Starr, Christopher Street, Marge Summit, Lucie Blue Tremblay, Jane Troxell, Robin Tyler, Jay Vail, Susan Waller, Cynthia White, Kathy Goodwin Wolfe, Susan Wolfe, and Sarah Wolfersberger. To the staff at Chicago *Outlines/ Nightlines*, both present and past; Women and Children First Bookstore; Brett and Carrie at People Like Us Bookstore; everyone at *Hot Wire*; Unabridged Books; and Michelle Karlsberg—thank you for your work in promoting lesbian writing, and Lesbomania in particular.

Thank you to Mountain Moving Coffeehouse and all the collective members and friends over the years, David Zak and the Bailiwick Theater's annual Lesbian and Gay Pride Series, the women of La Maison des Femmes (Paris), the Begine Cafe and Kultur Zentrum für Frauen (Berlin), Rhythm Fest Writers Series, The National Women's Music Festival, and the Lesbian and Gay Community Services Center of New York City, for hosting Lesbomania readings and slide shows.

Grateful thanks to the activists of ILGA, the International Lesbian and Gay Association, for their vital, ongoing work on behalf of lesbians and gay men everywhere.

Very special thanks to Sylvia B. Stallings, for her love, humor, intelligence, generous heart—and, among other things, for so deftly removing that satin ribbon from my bra with her teeth.

And to Sylvia, Jeannine, Karan, Carrie, Gina, and Deb, and the proprietors of the Check'er Inn women's guest house in Provincetown (their motto: "Check 'er out at the Check'er Inn"), for a truly lesbonic celebration of the New Year.

And last but definitely not least, sincere thanks to Claudia, Beth, and Dudley of New Victoria Publishers for their patience and faith in my work, and to Joan Hilty for so ably providing the visual whimsey.

Contents

Introduction

The columns in this collection were written between early 1990 and late 1993. The proliferation of lesbian images in the media that has occurred during this period—starting from almost zero to the cover of *Newsweek*—is a process that is fascinating to watch, and one that hopefully will continue to accelerate.

When I began writing Lesbomania, even the word "lesbian" was still rarely heard in any mainstream cultural venues.

To illustrate how quickly things are changing, just two weeks ago I read in the *Toronto Star*, a mainstream daily newspaper, that k.d. lang's lesbian-biker video from the movie *Even Cowgirls Get the Blues* was going to be banned from British television. *Not because it had a lesbian theme*—which it does—but because in it, lang and actress Uma Thurman ride a motorcycle without wearing safety helmets. The headline of this wry piece, "k.d. forced to practice safe cycling," explained that to circumvent the censors, two versions of the video have now been made: one with helmets and one without.

And that has solved the censorship problem, apparently.

In my early columns, I made a lot of fuss about the lack of lesbian presence on television and in the movies. At that time, you could still expect a call through your local lesbian phone tree to let you know if *anything* about lesbians was scheduled in TV listings or found on a program-in-progress: "Jorjet, hurry up, put on *Roseanne* right now!"

Now, thanks primarily to the TV talk shows, hardly a week goes by without some reference to lesbians—even if the context is one we are not thrilled about (last week's *Montel Williams*

1

show "Lesbians Who Beat Up Transsexuals" is just one min-uscule example). But at this point we can be fairly confident that if lesbians do anything remotely talk-show worthy, Mon-tel, or Oprah, or Sally Jessy, or Phil, or Geraldo and the others will do their best to milk it for all the sleazy air time it's worth.

And I appreciate that.

In mainstream movies, of course, we've gone from seeing one dreary suicidal-woman-in-denial-who-just-happens-to-be-a-you-know-what per decade to numerous clever, curva-ceous, unrepentant yuppie lesbians who just happen to be pathological.

But at least they're assertive.

Is this progress? Well, yeah, I think so. When I was a teenager there was NOTHING. No, I don't count Leslie Gore singing "You Don't Own Me" as a lesbian role model, though I know a few dykes who do—in retrospect.

Some of these columns could have been updated with new information, but I decided to leave them as they appeared when first published, as testimony to a particular time in our struggle, our progress, and our joy of discovery. When I wrote about Greta Garbo, for instance, I had not yet seen "A Woman of Affairs," an excellent presentation by Mary Wings and Eric Garber, that makes Garbo's lesbian life crystal clear. When I wrote about the importance of celebrities coming out of the closet, it was before k.d. lang and Melissa Etheridge broke the music business sound barrier.

Every lesbian who speaks out and tells her story adds to our understanding of what it means to be a lesbian—and changes, broadens that meaning. Nobody has a monopoly on what it is to be a lesbian. Lesbianism is not any single ideol-ogy, any more than lesbian sex is any single act, and woe to those who try to contain us. We are everywhere, and that means everywhere, all over the planet, trying to do the best we can to be true to ourselves.

We can draw strength from the courageous lesbians who live in places where it's not safe to be out, who even risk their lives to love other women. And from our courageous lesbian

2

foremothers whose names are sometimes known to us, most often not. And we can draw inspiration from our courageous lesbian contemporary artists and heroes.

Like Black filmmaker Michelle Parkerson, who has said, "Ours is the only revolution being fought for love."

Like Quebecois writer Nicole Brossard, who said, "The lesbian is living proof of women's genius. All women would like to believe in the 'genius' of women but only lesbians believe in it, take inspiration from it, live it."

Like Mexican poet Rosa-Maria Roffiel, who said, "We have served the sentence for daring to look at ourselves naked in front of the mirror; now let's run free."

Like Native American poet Chrystos, who said, "There are more of us than you can begin to believe."

Like severely disabled lesbian Sharon Kowalski, who said, "I am gay," and "I love you" by spelling out the words letter by letter on her alphabet board.

Like Black poet Pat Parker, who said, "In the act of loving each woman, I have learned a new lesson. I have learned to love myself."

Like Jewish lesbian comic and producer Robin Tyler, who said, back in 1979, "If you're straight then I'm crooked, but if I'm gay then you're morose."

And like Canadian singer k.d. lang, who advised other public figures, in *Rolling Stone:* "Being out is just great. I recommend it to people who are ready to do it. Just do it."

As I've defined it in one of my columns, *Lesbomania is being in love with being a lesbian.* After all these years, I'm still in love. And I've no doubt this romance will last for the rest of my life.

In fact, I believe that when lesbians everywhere are able to fully embrace freedom, power, and creativity in the world, that will be the beginning of the love affair of the *century*—the 21st century.

Jorjet Harper
Chicago, March 1994

3

A House is Not a Homo

The first word I ever heard used to refer to "gay" when I was a kid was "homo."

I was about eight. I noticed that my parents would sometimes mutter to each other, in a disparaging way, how "the homos" did this, and "the homos" were like that.

We lived in a tiny, run-down, rented tenement apartment in New York. When my parents spoke derisively about the "homos," I got the idea that they were talking about people who owned their own homes—that homo was short for *home-owner.*

I interpreted their negativity as jealousy. After all, who wouldn't want to be a homo? Homos had lots of room, sometimes little backyards and gardens. Some of the kids at school had parents who were homos. And there were quite a few homos living in row houses up the street.

My parents did own a television—and the TV shows were full of homos, too.

Father Knows Best, Leave It To Beaver—even *The Beverly Hillbillies* were homos. The only people who weren't homos were Lucy and Desi (and what a spectacular apartment they had by our standards) and the Kramdens on *The Honeymooners,* who lived in an apartment that looked kind of like ours, only their kitchen was a lot bigger.

Politicians, celebrities—it appeared that everybody who was anybody was a homo.

Eventually my misunderstanding of the word became apparent. I called a few married people homos, to my parents' horror, and they questioned me till they figured out what it was I had meant to say.

"Well, what *does* 'homo' mean, then?" I asked.

My parents looked at each other knowingly, as parents will do.

"It's a boy who likes boys," my mother said curtly, frowning.

Now, you will note at once the lesbian invisibility implicit in this euphemistic, misleading reply. Unlike Queen Victoria, my mother was well aware of the existence of lesbians—but more about that another time.

"Lots of boys like boys," I observed.

"No, no, she means *fairies*," said my father, making a face. "Homos are fairies." He puffed on his pipe as if that ended the matter.

Fairies? But I *loved* fairies! My favorite childhood story was Peter Pan. And when Tinkerbelle was dying, I clapped along with all the other kids, "I believe, I believe"—even though secretly I already had a doubt or two.

"Men who *act like* fairies," my mother clarified. "Queens."

"Fairy Queens?!" I shouted with enthusiasm.

"No! No!" my mother shouted back. "Look, just stop calling Mr. and Mrs. Hamby up the street 'homos,' alright?" she said sternly. "Don't use that word anymore. Don't ever use it again."

I sulked. "All right then," I said. "But if you won't explain what it means, and you won't let me say it, then you can't say it either. That's only fair."

Since my parents really didn't want to delve any more deeply into the subject than we had already, they agreed. There was no more talk about "the homos"—at least not in front of me.

They took the home out of homophobia, but not the homophobia out of the home.

We can be such complicated, perplexing creatures, we Homo sapiens.

Highway 61 Revisited

"So, what's it like to be a lesbian?" she asked me.

If it had been anybody but my old friend Randy, I might have thrown it right back at her and said: "What's it like to be straight?"

But the last time I saw Randy, I *was* straight—at least I thought I was. That was 22 years ago.

Our reunion took place in San Francisco, in the same place we'd met—North Beach, at the Cafe Trieste. Randy had been a "chick" of the late-beatnik-early-hippie variety, who knew all the most interesting, "far out" people in North Beach and Haight-Ashbury.

I was 18 when I met her. She was 25. She was worldly and funny and had done such *groovy* things. She'd lived at the infamous Greta Garbo Hotel. She was a personal friend of Owsley, the renegade LSD manufacturer. She was a firm advocate of "free love"—and had slept with more "cats" (archaic word for "dudes") than you could cram into a subway car.

In 1966 she had been my confidante, my role model, and, not incidentally, my very best source of hallucinogens.

We'd kept in touch all these years. Today, in what seems like another incarnation, she's an East Bay housewife, and I'm a lesbian journalist.

Randy still looks beautiful—but different. Her long, straight, honey-colored hair is grey-white and her face is deeply lined. We reminisced for hours over cappucino about our Love Generation days, and the crazy people we'd known. Us against the "squares." Letting our freak flag fly. We hadn't cared if people gave us dirty looks or said awful things about us. We were proud to be on the side of love, not war. We'd wanted a better, freer kind of world.

After awhile she pulled out a photo. "This is my husband Steve." A heavy-jowled man with a grey moustache wearing a floppy leather hat. He looked like Jerry Garcia.

"He's ten years younger than me," she said.

I pulled out a photo of my lover in her motorcycle jacket.

"She's twelve years younger than me," I said.

Randy sighed. "So many of my old friends are gay now," she said wistfully.

"Mine too," I said, rather more enthusiastically.

I showed her copies of a few of the gay and lesbian newspapers I write for, and told her about the gay and lesbian conference I was covering—my main reason for being in San Francisco.

"It kind of amazes me that there's even such a thing now as a 'gay and lesbian' community," she volunteered. "I mean, it's great, but it's strange, too. To me, gay men and lesbians have always seemed so different from each other."

"Well, it's not like there aren't any problems," I said, about to embark on my standard gay-culture/lesbian-culture rap. "I think there are certain stereotypes that go very far back. One of them is the old stereotype that lesbians hate men, you know, that they think all men are pigs...."

"Men *are* pigs, Jorjet," she interrupted. "Take it from me, let me tell you. Men are really pigs."

My former Acid Goddess then launched into a bitter half-hour diatribe about her cheating, do-nothing husband, and went on to enumerate the crimes and infidelities of a long series of ex-lovers. I hadn't heard such vehement anti-male talk in years, not even from ultra-radical separatists. I was shocked.

"So," she said, taking a deep breath after getting all this venom out of her system, "What's it like to be a lesbian?"

What could I say? Where could I possibly begin?

Finally, looking up from my cup of cappucino, I said, "Well, it's kind of like being a hippie. Only a lot...groovier." I smiled. She smiled, too—that old twinkly-eyed Randy smile I remembered from years ago.

"Far out," she said.

Read My Lips

Okay, so what exactly is "lesbomania," anyway?

As we know, mainstream documentation is a little slow on the uptake when it comes to anything gay and lesbian—unless it's something negative. Not only hasn't "lesbomania" found its way into the thesaurus yet, but I expect it will be quite awhile before it hits the dictionary.

Some supposedly contemporary dictionaries haven't even discovered that there is more than a sexual definition for the word "lesbian" yet.

They're still thinking with their gonads, as H.L. Mencken used to say.

But since I invented the word "lesbomania," at least I get first dibs at defining it.

lesbomania: 1.) An overwhelming interest in all things pertaining to lesbians. 2.) Elevation of mood, enthusiasm, and pulse rate at the thought or mention of anything relating to lesbians. 3.) An extreme form of lesbophilia. 4.) A euphoric phase in the coming out process for many lesbians.

In short, lesbomania is being in love with being a lesbian.

And let's not forget the subject of this pleasant, desirable condition:

lesbomaniac: 1.) A lesbian characterized by an inordinate enthusiasm for all things pertaining to lesbians. 2.) A lesbian who is gifted with or inspired by lesbomania.

You'll notice that by my definition, non-lesbians cannot be true lesbomaniacs.

By the way, the opposite of "lesbomania" is "lesbophobia."

Webster's and *Oxford* and *American Heritage*, are you paying attention? Of course not. But you will need these definitions more than lesbians will. Because, I've been delighted to discover, a lot of lesbians understand what "lesbomania" means without needing to have it defined.

Many women have been through that explosion of lesbonic energy that happens while coming out. That craving to find out everything and anything about lesbians. To read voraciously anything you can find on the subject. To check out all the cobwebby old women's music albums and research gay and lesbian history. To go anywhere you might possibly meet other lesbians, once you've figured out you are one.

For some women, lesbomania is a phase. For others, it's a way of life.

You will know that you're a major lesbomaniac when you are firmly convinced—

...despite all the evidence that many dykes are just as fucked up as straight people...

...despite all the sleazy, hypocritical politicians who are openly homophobic and secretly gay...

...despite all the celebrity queers who think they have more to lose by coming out than a woman with three kids who works in a factory...

...despite all the nasty trashing and occasional open warfare between different factions in the lesbian community...

...despite all the ex-lovers with whom we may barely be on speaking terms...

—that lesbians are the most brilliant and interesting people in the world.

Because we are.

And I can tell you why.

Lesbians are the most brilliant and interesting people in the world because we have figured out who we are, and found each other, and built communities, and fostered our own culture, despite all of society's incessant messages that there is not and cannot be any such thing, that we cannot and do not exist.

And yet not only do we exist, we are flourishing.

Now, is that brilliant or what? So maybe I'm a little brash, a little zealous. But let's not underestimate the value and importance of lesbomania in a world where lesbians are not even supposed to happen, much less be happy about being our fabulous lesbian selves.

Yay! Give me an L...! Give me an E...!

Beyond the Straight and Narrow

There's been a lot of discussion in the gay and lesbian community about whether or not influential people who are gay but who actively work against gay rights should be dragged kicking and screaming out of their moth-eaten, pathetic little closets. Many people see it as an important ethical issue that needs to be approached with great care.

Meantime, though, *The Enquirer*, *The Star*, and the rest of the tabloid press newspapers are tossing people out of the closet with the vigor of a trampoline act.

And aren't we delighted when they do?

While politicians and movie stars and pop singers cringe at being labelled gay, we anticipate the thrill of discovering another member of the tribe.

When Chastity Bono came out, even my mother was happy—she felt that at last she had something in common with Cher.

Then Chas denied it all. Oh well. My mother would just as soon I denied it, too—another thing she and Cher probably have in common.

How we all love the Guess Who Game. "Guess who I heard was gay?" someone says, and this little tingle of anticipation travels up your spine.

Weren't you thrilled when you heard that Elizabeth McGovern, Jamie Lee Curtis, and Olivia Newton-John are dykes, *whether it's true or not?* Wasn't it fun the first time you heard that Tom Selleck, John Travolta, and Richard Chamberlain were queer? *Whether you like them or not?*

Well, of course it's classier to come out on your own, like Sir John Gielgud or Barney Frank or Martina Navratilova. You not only gain some small amount of control in how your personal life is presented to the public, you gain the instant respect of at least ten percent of the population.

There are a few gays I would prefer to hear were straight, however. If *The Enquirer* broke the story that J. Edgar Hoover was really heterosexual after all, I wouldn't feel any sense of loss. Ditto for Roy Cohn.

And as far as I'm concerned, all major homophobes who may secretly be gay—as witness recent rumors about Jesse Helms, for example—those people shouldn't just be tossed out of the closet, they should be tossed into a salad. Literally.

But what can you do? As a friend's kindly mother said to her when she came out, "Just remember, dear, that not all gay people are good."

Does it bother you, as *The Star* reported last week, that Kristy McNichol barks like a dog before having sex with her girlfriend? Not me. Heck no. I'm a dog lover.

In fact, I'm so glad to hear she's a dyke that now I'm willing to watch all those wretched TV episodes she was in that I managed to avoid squandering my time on through the years.

Actually, though, I'd much rather go to that lesbian party *The Star* claims "super butch" Kristy regularly drops in on— the one *The Star* says goes on in Century City round-the-clock.

Tell me: where exactly?

Of course, it's a measure of our oppression that to be "labelled" gay or lesbian is still seen as a severe stigma or taint. Recently in one of the tabloids, Arsenio Hall lamented being "charged with" being gay. He said he wasn't gay, and to call someone gay when they aren't is "nasty."

We live in a society that thinks it's nasty to call someone gay when they are, too. Nobody goes around pointing at politicians and celebrities saying, "We suspect you of being straight, and we're going to leak it to the press."

So I say let's start tossing everybody out of the closet, whether they are gay or not. Assume everybody is gay, till they "prove" otherwise.

Straight people see the world in that skewed, self-centered perspective, so why shouldn't we?

And why shouldn't straight people put some energy into having to protest the assumptions made about their sex lives, emotional lives, and social lives, for a change?

Call it "turning the table-oids."

And if some of them aren't really gay or lesbian after all, *why shouldn't they be flattered we thought they were?*

I'd like to see Oprah Winfrey dispel rumors that she's a lesbian by telling the press, "Well, no, as a matter of fact, I'm not a lesbian, though I realize that people might think so because I'm such an independent, self-assured, charming, intelligent woman."

I'd like Arsenio Hall, on his national TV show seen by umpteen millions, to address the "nasty" rumors that he's gay. He could flash that Tim Curry smile of his, stare straight at the camera, and say, "About those rumors. No, I'm not gay—but I can see why you might suspect I am, since I'm one of the most talented, charming, and successful people in show business."

And wouldn't we all love Elizabeth Taylor, if, "accused" of being a lesbian because she played cupid for Rock Hudson and Malcolm Forbes (figure that one out), she told *The Star*, "No, honestly, I'm not a lesbian, but where there's life there's hope, so hey, who knows?"

Tension Mounts at Beaver Dam
A Special News Report

BEAVER DAM, WISCONSIN—The atmosphere is tense here this evening as long-time butch patrons of the infamous Huggybear Lounge have threatened to turn the legendary role-playing bar into a "femme-free space."

The Huggybear Lounge has been a butch/femme landmark for an incredible 47 years. From the outside, it appears to be a nondescript clapboard structure sandwiched between a pizza shop and a Wal-Mart near the bustling business district off the exit ramp of Highway 151.

But for those who knew of the existence of this secret underground butch/femme mecca, nighttime turned the Huggybear into a sapphic sanctuary.

Many lesbians in the 1970s and '80s felt time had passed the Huggybear by. It was only through the vision and personal charisma of its owner, lifelong stone butch Dusty O'Toole, that the Huggybear weathered the hard times and survived—albeit as a lone, almost forgotten outpost in the hard-core butch/femme wilderness.

But recently, a noticeable lack of good will had been discernable between the bar's butch and femme regulars. Many reported that a crankiness, a tendency to argue, had been growing—a trend indicating that some women were rubbing each other the wrong way.

Relations turned starkly ugly last week, as the appearance of lesbian sex counselor JoAnn Loulan in nearby Madison drew protesting butches from several counties. Radical butch agitators, picketing the event, charged that as a femme Loulan always has the "option of passing for straight."

Trouble escalated further last Monday with the announcement that a radical femme vegetarian group based in Oshkosh, the Lesboterians, would organize a nationwide picket of butcher shops. Radical butches interpreted this as a retaliatory counter-attack, believing they were the hidden targets of the veggie-femme protest.

This week, angry Huggybear butches announced that as of April 1, the Huggybear would become a "femme-free space."

"I don't understand how things could have come to this," said O'Toole, who is sympathetic with the butch cause but reluctant to turn away femmes at the door.

"Yeah, so butches get shit on more in society—but here at the Huggybear, femmes are second-class citizens," complained Trixie Wilcox, a femme for 34 years. "'Oh, you look so butch!' everybody sez, and that's always a compliment. Who ever sez, 'Oh, you look so femme!' and means it in a *nice* way?"

"We got tired of all the screeching, that's all," said Rocky Tweezer, a Huggybear patron for over 10 years. "We want to watch our sports shows in peace. A bar is no place for a femme anyway. If they want their own turf, they should take over a beauty parlor."

"I didn't become a lesbian just to be treated like a straight woman all over again," countered one bitter femme (who asked that her name not be printed), when told she would be barred from the bar. "I *love* butches—I mean, I'm a *femme*, for chrissakes!—but the bunch we got here in Beaver Dam are no better than generic men."

Yesterday, in a move that may set the stage for an escalation of the conflict, Huggybear butches issued a manifesto, bragging that in any hands-on confrontation, femmes were sure to surrender with their hands up, and the butches would win hands down.

But bar owner O'Toole was not confident of any quick victory for the cocky butches. "This is a terrible situation, just terrible," she lamented. "And before it's all over, I think both sides may be in for a serious licking."

Fighting Erupts Between Butches and Femmes
A Special News Update

BEAVER DAM, WISCONSIN—Burly butches and furious femmes battled it out in hand-to-hand combat for control of the Huggybear Lounge here after butches made good on their April First threat to declare the famous hard-core role-playing bar a "femme-free space" and began ejecting femmes from the premises. Stunned mall shoppers, huddled in nearby store-fronts, watched as dozens of lesbians with beehive hairdos, some wearing prom-style gowns with spaghetti straps and glitter pumps, were roughly pushed out the door of the bar. Some of the femmes staggered around the parking lot in shock, their lovely dresses sweat-soaked and beer-stained.

A few butch bar patrons, too, were mystified. "Exc-yoo-ooze me, but aren't butches and femmes supposed to *like* each other?" groaned Huggybear pool champion Spike Martini, who said she had been unaware of any growing discord in the bar, and was frustrated that her tournament game had been interrupted by the fighting.

Yet other Huggybear regulars claim that as long as six months ago, they knew a problem existed. Several admit that animosity had risen to such a pitch that sex-role-playing spies from both camps, along with crossover accomplices, had been engaging in intensive undercover activities.

"I had no idea this gorgeous butch I'd picked up at the Huggybear was really a total femme in disguise!" said one despondent femme who refused to give her name. "By the time I realized my mistake, it was too late—I'd revealed everything! Now I have to ask myself," she said, sobbing, "Will I ever be able to trust again?"

Part-time bartender Bobo Weed and bar owner Dusty O'Toole said they felt they had been making progress in

16

negotiating with butches to retract their recent anti-femme manifesto. But at a critical stage, their efforts were ruined by one intoxicated bar patron who kept taunting the femmes, shouting "Butches are the dykes with balls, femmes are only Barbie dolls!"

"That's when the fake fur really started to fly," said Weed. "Some femmes got a little bit hysterical, and then butches began shoving them all out the door."

"It was horrible, just like the Wild West," said femme Lily Good. "When people started throwing chairs, I ran. I mean, I'm not one of those *radical* femmes, I'm a, uh, a *real* femme. Absolutely. My friend Babs tried to stay, and she broke a heel and fell down when they pushed her out. Luckily she was wearing this enormous crinoline slip that cushioned her fall. Her hair was such a mess! I was terrified. *Absolutely.*"

"These two butches strong-armed me right out of the place," said Kiki Sweet, who had fought to remain in the bar. "It was intense. I mean, there was ripped lace everywhere. Look at me, I'm all smudged. I broke a nail. First time I've ever scratched a butch standing up," she said breathlessly.

Asked if they believed the femmes had just cause to fight for their right to remain in the Huggybear, Good and Sweet linked arms and shouted what has become one of the cheers of the outraged femmes: "4-6-8-10, butches are as bad as men!"

Chants of "Huggybear or Bust!" continued to echo across the mall parking lot adjacent to the bar this evening as the femmes and their gathering supporters, staging a rally, now threaten to storm the bar.

"We're pissed now, babe!" said a flushed Sweet, quivering with excitement. "Wait'll I get my hands on 'em—I know a couple of butches who're gonna have very swollen lips before I'm through with them. They're gonna need mound-to-mound resuscitation."

Femmes Penetrate Butch Stronghold
A Special News Update

BEAVER DAM, WISCONSIN—A mob of fired-up femmes, wielding farm implements purchased at a nearby feed store and tools borrowed from local gas stations, broke down the barricaded door of the Huggybear Lounge in an effort to regain control of the landmark role-playing bar from which they had been banned by butches.

Some two hundred femmes and their supporters also brandished stuffed bears; the symbol of their struggle, and shouted cries of "Huggybear or Bust!"

Fighting quickly spilled back outside the bar to the nearby mall parking lot as butches lunged out, attempting to harness the femme surge. Noontime shoppers gaped as more than a hundred women in motorcycle jackets and women in pastel frocks chased each other around parked cars, threw popcorn and other food at each other, wrestled each other to the ground, and, more often than not, eventually collapsed, panting, into each other's arms.

By the battle's end, there was still no clear-cut victor, and many butches who identified as "femmy butch" and femmes who identified as "butchy femme" expressed confusion as to which side they were on.

Two lesbians from nearby Cowpat Junction also witnessed the battle.

"I was not inside the bar. I want to make that very clear. I don't go to bars," said Artemisia Earthsister, 37. "In fact, I don't like to come into town at all, because it upsets my karma. But now and then we need to buy bird seed to bring back to Mammary Farm—that's the commune where I live with my sister dykes and we grow organic soybeans—because we need to feed our sister ducks and wild sisterbirds."

"We had just stopped to get some refreshing non-diet, non-carbonated natural fruit beverages and saw this—how can I describe it—this *scene*," said Earthsister's companion, Gynika Wombwomoon, 42. "Frankly, I was appalled. At the farm we have evolved beyond role-playing, and practice strict equality in all of our sexual sharing. And here were all these screaming women, dressed in totally polarized *costumes*, some even made of non-biodegradable materials! And they were running around *grabbing* at each other!"

"At first we assumed it was some weird new lesbian spring equinox ritual thing," said Earthsister. "Then someone explained to us that it was actually happening spontaneously. We can't tell you how deeply such behavior oppresses us. At Mammary Farm it would never be tolerated."

As word of the conflict spread quickly through the lesbian grapevine, lesbian evangelist Tanya Jensen showed up to address the throng. Jensen is the author of the controversial book *Getting Out of Love's Slime*, in which she theorizes that all sexual desire is a sadomasochistic plot perpetrated by capitalist hegemonic patriarchy.

Speaking from atop a flatbed truck, Jensen attributed all "horizontal hostility between lesbians" to their "stubborn tendency to engage in sexual activity," and shouted through a bullhorn: "My Sisters! Passion is an addictive drug! Break the cycle and be saved!"

Flush-faced butches and femmes, who continued to throw popcorn, beer, clothing, and shoes at each other with increasing playfulness, paid no attention to Jensen's plea.

Who now lays claim to the disputed Huggybear turf? One exhausted but happy femme waved her stuffed teddy toward the crowd in triumph as she was regally escorted back into the bar after surrendering to a befuddled butch she had tackled to the parking lot pavement moments earlier.

"At this point," she giggled, "I'd say everything is up for grabs."

Negotiations Open at Beaver Dam
A Special News Update

BEAVER DAM, WISCONSIN—Longtime lesbian superstar and community mediator Alix Dobkin was flown into the Beaver Dam war zone from New York this afternoon to hammer out a peace treaty between the fighting butch and femme factions of the legendary hard-core role-playing bar, the Huggybear Lounge.

Landing by helicopter directly onto the roof of the bar, Dobkin was taken immediately to the conference table downstairs—a hastily converted pool table—by anxious representatives from both sides in the conflict.

The decision to call Dobkin in to mediate was made after local police chief Edwin "Big Ed" Dolittle announced he would not directly attempt to intervene in the crisis unless there was danger of injury to innocent bystanders.

"I'm not gonna get in the middle of this, no way," he said. "It's not my culture. Since this is an internal conflict between warring factions of Lesbian Nation, my department has no jurisdiction."

Thus it appears that Beaver Dam, Wisconsin, has become the first United States municipality to officially recognize the sovereignty of the Lesbian State.

But haggard bar owner stone butch Dusty O'Toole was not cheered by this news. "So what the fuck does that do? Forty-seven years in business, we manage to keep a nice low profile," she said at the Huggybear's rear loading dock as she helped unload a shipment of frozen corn dogs during a break in negotiations. "Now every friggin' homo-hating pig farmer between here and Kokomo's gonna try to boot my ass outta here."

O'Toole's anxiety was quickly calmed, however, as she was

20

approached by owners of neighboring shops in the mall. So much food, pizza, soda, candy, and other items have been sold so far during the crisis—the mall's Wal-Mart has sold over three hundred stuffed bears alone to fervent femme supporters—that local mall merchants have joined forces to present O'Toole with a proposal to re-enact what some are now calling the "new butch/femme mating ritual" each weekend during the summer tourist season. The proposed package, including a generous advertising budget, would make the Huggybear an official Beaver Dam tourist attraction.

Next door to the Huggybear, pizza shop owner Giuseppi Scarpia says that he plans to convert his fast-food restaurant into a role-playing theme bar for straight people. "Why should these lovely gay ladies have *all* the fun?" he quipped.

Whether the straight people would reverse roles or stay in the ones they've already got was not yet clear.

Local merchants' optimistic reaction to the recent events appears to be shared by at least some other local residents—most of whom had no idea the Huggybear even existed until the butch-femme conflict erupted April 1 when butches declared the Huggybear a "femme-free space."

"I don't know if them gals was drunk or just upset, but gol-lee, they dress mighty fine," said Mabel Greenley, 73, wife of a local dairy farmer, who was shopping at the nearby Wal-Mart when the fighting broke out. Greenley has joined the vigil outside the bar as a town watches and waits with bated breath to see if Dobkin's peace initiative will be successful.

"By cracky, I never knew you could be a lesbian and still wear a dress, or I'da given it some thought myself when I was young and spunky," Greenley said. "Might be I'll give it a try yet," she added, winking.

Calm Restored at Beaver Dam
A Special News Update

BEAVER DAM, WISCONSIN—After intense negotiations behind closed doors at the legendary role-playing mecca, the Huggybear Lounge, feuding butches and femmes emerged along with bar owner Dusty O'Toole and negotiator Alix Dobkin, to announce to the waiting crowd that the two sides had come to a "happy truce" after their stormy conflict of recent weeks.

How did peacemaker Dobkin, who had been flown into Beaver Dam expressly to hammer out a settlement between warring butches and femmes, manage to defuse the explosive conflict?

"During the early stages of the negotiations, the butch representatives and I established our butch bonds, while at the same time I exchanged a little flirtation with the femme representatives. That way we established a certain level of comfort in the negotiation process," said Dobkin, adding that most of the lesbians involved in the conflict had had a great time, "Especially," she said, "the ones who got the most upset."

After hearing the complaints of both sides, Dobkin said she realized the problem was all based on several misunderstandings, which she simply cleared up.

"I explained to the butches that when the vegetarian femmes picketed butcher shops it was not meant as a reflection on them. I reminded the femmes that butches by nature are very tenderhearted and wouldn't really harm a living creature. And I explained that I am also a former heterosexual, and butches shouldn't think of femmes as being less lesbian than they are—it takes all kinds of lesbians to make a community."

Then, said Dobkin, "We did an ancient lesbian ritual, originally designed to unearth the hidden attributes of butches to bring out their tender softness, and the femmes to develop their most positive take charge qualities which many femmes (known as Take-Charge Femmes or TCFs) are famous for."

Without divulging details, Dobkin said that such rituals have only two elements: "One, we have to have fun, and the other, we have to make it up as we go. And a spiritual transformation occurred, which nobody expected or planned for: we realized we can get anything we want in the world with a complete, integrated lesbian personality, each in her own unique way. And we devised a strategy—you might call it 'Walking softly with a big schtick'—by which butches and femmes, tapping into all this true deep dyke energy, will eventually take over the world."

"Finally," said Dobkin, "we butches and femmes all raised our voices and sang *I Did It My Way* as a two-part *a capella* round, and there wasn't a dry eye in the place."

"Thank goddess it's all over," said a bleary-eyed staff member of the influential journal *Lesbian Connection*, upon hearing of the truce. For their upcoming issue, LC has been forced to add an additional twelve full sheets to their regular bundle of pages just to print the flood of opinions they have received so far relating to the Beaver Dam Crisis. "We even had to buy a stapler that would take longer staples just because of this situation," she said.

The Huggybear story has also grabbed the interest of mainstream media. Ted Koppel will reportedly examine the butch/femme conflict on an upcoming ABC *Nightlines* program, to be entitled "Showdown at Beaver Dam," in which he will pose hard-hitting questions about sex roles to Phil Donahue, who will appear as spokesperson for the lesbian community.

Time Magazine is considering a cover story on the Huggybear, and *Newsweek* has announced it will begin featuring a special lesbian section (possibly a pull-out) as part of its regular coverage.

"We had no idea lesbians were doing such interesting things right under our noses," said columnist Liz Smith.

Back in Beaver Dam, everything seems quiet again—but what of the future? Will Dobkin's peace initiative last? And if so, will butches and femmes actually take over the world? As the butches and femmes regroup, spokesdykes for both sides are reluctant to speculate about what may happen next. The Old Timers in particular are well aware that, especially in wartime, loose lips can sink ships.

Kissing Cousins

My lover had to go into the hospital for surgery. She introduced me to her doctor: "This is my lover."

He didn't bat an eyelash, just smiled and shook my hand the way anybody would if we lived in a non-homophobic society.

Score one for Lesbian Visibility.

The nurses all reacted well, too. If homosexuality was an issue for them, they managed to hide it nicely.

Score another for Lez-Viz.

On the day of my lover's operation, however, Lesbian Visibility hit just a bit of a snag in the hospital waiting room.

Guarding the door was an elderly woman with blue-tinted hair and thick rhinestone-framed glasses. In a bureaucratic manner she began what was obviously an often-repeated speech: "Waiting for a surgery patient? Please take a seat here and make yourself comfortable. When the patient is able to see visitors, I will inform you."

She had a ledger book in front of her. "What is the patient's last name?" she asked.

I told her.

"Could you spell that for me, please?"

I did—slowly, because I saw that she was wearing a hearing aid and seemed to be watching my lips.

She flipped through a few pages, found the name, and put a check mark next to it. Then, her pen poised above a blank space, she asked: "And what is your relation to the patient?"

Lesbian Visibility time. "I'm her lover," I said.

Though the word "lover" seemed to echo through the big waiting room to every husband, wife, child, aunt, and uncle sitting around reading magazines, the blue-haired lady appeared not to have heard me.

She looked up over the top of her eyeglasses. "Excuse me?"

"I'm her lover," I repeated, slowly.

She just stared at me.

"Her Significant Other," I tried, though it occurred to me as soon as I'd said it that maybe "significant other" would only confuse rather than clarify the situation for this lady. She looked back down at her ledger book, puzzled, thinking. After a long pause, she slowly wrote, in a large, quavering, round script, the word *cousin*.

"Thank you," she said, smiling, and waved me on into the waiting room.

I dutifully took a seat to begin my vigil.

But inside, I was fuming. I ran over the incident in my mind. The exasperating thing was, I simply could not decide if the woman had heard me right or not.

"Lover" and "other" and "cousin" sound *sort of* alike, don't they?

Well, then "husband" sort of sounds like "cousin," too—did she make husbands into cousins in her ledger book?

Or maybe she'd heard me perfectly but thought she was doing me a favor by making me a relative by some conventional definition?

Nope, I thought, straight people *want* us to lie about our relationships so *they* don't have to deal with it. Okay. All right. The next time something like this happens, I'll do it *their* way. I'll just lie. I'll say "*wife*," and see how that one goes over. And if they balk at that, I'll lie some more, and say we were married in Denmark....

When my lover was out of surgery, the blue-haired lady, still perfectly pleasant, told me how to find the intensive care unit.

Happily, my lover was doing well, and the reunited "cousins" kissed in an especially loving, Significant-Otherly way.

Lesbian Visibility was back on track.

But I left the hospital that evening still wondering if my lover had become my cousin through homophobia, or bureaucratic conformity, or merely because of a low battery in someone's hearing aid.

When Things of the Spirit Come First

I don't identify as either butch or femme.

Such a "confession" may or may not be sacrilege these days, depending on your religion.

Please understand that I'm not saying I think there's anything wrong with calling yourself butch or femme. In fact, I think butch/femme distinctions are a really interesting aspect of lesbian culture. I just don't personally feel I'm definitively one or the other, as I understand the meaning of the terms.

Like many dykes, I often find it fun and convenient and even logical to sort things into butch/femme dichotomies and to ponder butch/femme differences. And I know that the terms are very real for the butches and femmes who do identify as one or the other.

But I don't believe, as some lesbians do, that butchness and femmeness are "innate." Nor do I believe, as New Agey lesbian sex therapist JoAnn Loulan claims, that butch/femme is an "archetype" from the lesbian "collective unconscious."

For some women, the butch/femme "mystique" has approached a kind of religious mysticism. So I guess it was inevitable that some dykes somewhere would come up with a literal butch/femme religion. But the ones who have, a lesbian couple in Galena, Kansas, are far from being New Agers; they're devout fundamentalist Christians.

That's right. They claim that the Word of the Lord has been revealed to them through prayer, and it contains a Christian theological explanation for the difference between "butch" and "femme." They proclaim their Good Word in a headline:

Amazing Revelation: Lesbians' Origin Revealed.

A little redundant, but that's the least of their problems.

First of all, these women preach that it's lesbians who are really the "Chosen People."

Now, I grant you that's a feeling I've often had myself, as a lesbomaniac. But they go quite a bit further down the religious primrose path than I would ever venture:

"Lesbians are on earth in a physical body today for the specific purpose of gaining and bringing forth a new type of life, one that is free of evil, suffering, sickness, and death."

I'm not making this up; I'm quoting from their newsletter.

They say butches and femmes have different "Spiritual Origins." Some dykes are "Born Lesbians" (butches, naturally) and are really "Heavenly Spirit Beings" who have incarnated on Earth. Others "become" lesbians during their lifetime (that's how they define femme) and these lesbians are the descendants of Lucifer (the Devil, in case you forgot), who was cast out of Heaven, as they put it, "because of his desire to be an individual."

Hmmm. That's as reasonable an explanation for butch/femme as any other I've heard. To define butches as the "born lesbians" is kind of predictable, but the daughters-of-Lucifer femme thing is quite a creative touch. Very Original.

And the gals from Galena don't stop there. They claim that God created lesbians and gays before straight people. *Heterosexuality* started up in the first place because of the constant need the Devil's femmy descendants had for "new bodies."

Hence the need for breeders...

Sounds like these Uber-femmes were sort of celestial clothes horses, with an insatiable fashion demand to inhabit new bodies every season. (Ann Rice could do a whole series of novels about supernatural femme body thieves.)

Back to the butches: the capital B Butches, the Heavenly Spirit Beings, came to Earth as a result of the femme infiltration, specifically to "rescue souls from wallowing any further in their heterosexuality."

Yes, that's right, from *wallowing in their heterosexuality*. (I'm Saved!)

But the main mission of the Butches on Earth is not just to rescue hets (which might, all in all, be a thankless task), but to lead everyone—gay and straight and bi—to a "higher spiritual path."

One in which nobody has any sex at all.

I suppose we should have known: Sex is still the big bugaboo, the source of all sin, in a fundamentalist Christian lesbian cosmology—even one in which butches are angels and femmes are, um, devilettes.

Granted, I've certainly known some butches who could be angelic at times....

All lesbians, according to the fundamentalist logic, are apparently "closer to the Spirit," though, because lesbians, say the couple from Galena, have less sex than either gay men or straight people. And the highest kind of lesbians, either butch or femme, they say, are those who have gone through menopause (as they have) and (consequently, they say) have a diminished sex drive.

This may be the first fundamentalist Christian explanation for that waning of desire known as "lesbian bed death."

Another interesting twist—and a bit of an influence from the New Agers after all—is that the Heavenly Butch Spirit Beings, like the Fiery Femmes, have supposedly gone through many incarnations to get to where they are today. And before they were incarnated as butches, they were incarnated as gay men.

Yes, the *original* Original Angelic Spirit Beings were gay men. In other words—if I understand correctly the cosmology these women are preaching—all butch lesbians alive on the planet today were gay men in a former lifetime.

How do you like them apples, Evie?

"Many incarnations later, these male homosexuals became 'raised' a degree." They realized their penises were "keeping them separated from the Spirit." A group of these gay men (we don't know what group or how many) "offered up their desire for sex, and renounced the penis, which enabled them to be born in female bodies."

I'm still quoting from their newsletter, so help me goddess.

But there is still a glitch in the heavenly plan: even after the penis-renouncing Spirit Being gay men (not to be confused with transsexuals, I suppose) were born in female bodies, "heterosexual blood still flowed in their veins."

I'm fuzzy on the logic of this point. If they were gay angels to begin with, where did their "heterosexual blood" come from? (But maybe I'm being picky; maybe it's one of those questions you just don't ask, like wondering where Cain's wife came from.)

And though being gay might have some genetic component, since when do straight people and gay people have different kinds of *blood*? It sounds so authentically medieval.

But to finish the Greatest Story Ever Told, these Spirit Being gay men who renounced their penises were "now incarnated as females." But this heterosexual blood that somehow still flowed in their veins is the reason that these former-gay-male *women* now "found themselves attracted to women."

I see that Christian Lesbian Theology can get very complex. Like, how many butch Angel Spirit Beings can dance on the head of a pin? I'm not very clear on where Jesus fits into this cosmology, either, unless he's one of the gay penis-renouncers who are now butch dykes dedicated to saving the world from sex. And what are all the ramifications of this penis-renouncing gay-to-butch angel business? For example, does this mean that dykes who like to wear dildos are spiritual backsliders?

The bottom line on all this: The gals from Galena claim that the "conflicting angelic and demonic heavenly origins of lesbians" is the real reason "lesbians tend to argue so much."

So the next time you get annoyed at your lover for not

flushing the toilet or whatever, you must realize that what's really going on is an underlying spiritual conflict. Remember the old pop song from the Sixties: "Devil or Angel, dear whichever you are, I love you..."

And the Galena Gals say that this conflicting celestial origin also explains why "there is so much turmoil in the lives of lesbian couples."

I gather that dyke home life in Galena can be a bit rocky at times.

I wonder if they sing hymns out there, too, like "Dyke of Ages, Cleft for Me..."

But despite my skepticism, I have to tip my hat to these two lesbians in Galena, Kansas, for giving our community, at long last, a cosmological framework for the "innate" nature of butch/femme relationships. The next time I argue theology with a Christian, I'll be sure to lay this theory on 'im.

Still I'm mighty glad, Toto, that you and I don't live in Kansas anymore.

Godzilla Emerges From The Closet

Have there ever been times when straight people made you feel like you were some kind of monster from the murky depths?

When someone turns beet red, stammers "Ohhh! Yoooou're a lezzzzbian?!" and runs away in panic, it can make you feel kind of, well, queer.

Their odd behavior can be explained, however, by what I call "The Godzilla Theory of Social Acceptance."

Remember Godzilla? He was a 400-foot tall prehistoric reptile who slumbered under the ocean for millions of years, then woke up and stalked Tokyo, squashing people with his giant clawed feet and knocking over bridges and buildings. Godzilla was a box office hit in 1956.

In popular culture, familiarity breeds not contempt but affection. So by the fourth or fifth movie sequel, the monster Godzilla had become a good guy, fighting to save the world.

We began to understand him. He hadn't meant to frighten anybody or slow up traffic, he was just disoriented from all those centuries underwater, and depressed because people seemed so afraid of him.

Godzilla became likeable. He was on our side. He even looked kind of cute with that wobbly polyurethane tail.

Now consider. For hundreds of years homosexual people have been denounced—when we were located at all—as freaks, strange and incomprehensible, dangerous sexual sinners, almost as mythological monsters.

Then comes Stonewall, and like Godzilla rising out of the sea, we become truly visible for the first time—to ourselves and to others.

We realize we have power, and we don't have to fall for all the shit the straight world believes about us.

But what about the straight world? They still see us as some kind of menacing monsters, bent on destroying what crooked politicians call "the fabric of society" (another myth). The makers of *Godzilla* knew that scary monsters sell. The publishers of newspapers know this, too, and they've begun cashing in on homophobia in a big way. The words "gay" and "lesbian" are suddenly popping up in tabloid headlines everywhere.

This isn't "outing," it's capitalist sensationalism.

But brace yourself, Hollywood. The Lavender Menace is now creeping across Tinseltown like the shadow of Godzilla falling over Tokyo Bay.

Every week another star—Chamberlain, Garbo, Travolta, Bowie, Jagger, Cher's daughter, Streisand's son, even Elvis— is being linked with the scary G and L words.

Now, according to my Godzilla Theory, the more those scary words crop up in popular culture—especially when attached to *celebrities who we know aren't monsters*—the more accepted we'll be.

It doesn't even ultimately matter if these stars deny it or not—the subject is finally being discussed, considered as possible. And straight people will thus eventually feel less threatened, more empathetic—even able to say the G and L words themselves without fear or malice.

Will my Godzilla Theory hold true?

I don't know. If it does, in a few years we won't be treated like hideous 400-foot mutant reptiles anymore. We'll shrink to human size and be considered different, but good guys—like Mutant Ninja Turtles.

Hollywood might go for that in a big way.

High Visibility

My friend Michèle brought her German lover Anja to meet me for dinner at the Staropolska Restaurant. Anja had arrived from Berlin just two days before, for a brief visit. Talk about LIP (the "Lesbian Insanity Period"), they were IN IT DEEP. They couldn't keep their hands off each other. And why should they have to?

The Staropolska is a dyed-in-the-wool West Side Chicago Polish restaurant, with a largely Polish clientele, and wispy young waitresses who speak English with a Polish accent. It's a bit of a trek out there, but the all-you-can-eat Polish buffet for $4.50 is a real deal. And I thought Anja, being German, might have a taste for some sausage and sauerkraut.

But Anja and Michèle hardly noticed the food. They kissed so passionately so often that the sauerkraut and kielbasa and potatoes grew cold on their plates.

I mean *passionately*. They weren't horizontal on the vinyl booth bench or anything, and there was no breast-groping or disrobing going on, but they were seriously making up for lost time since Michèle got back to the U.S. from Berlin three months earlier.

You might say it was a kind of spontaneous two-woman Lesbian Kiss-In at the Polish buffet.

I should also mention that both Anja and Michèle have very butch haircuts—only Anja's is more spiked, with a maroon streak. Both are very tall and statuesque. And both wore black turtlenecks, black jeans, and black leather jackets.

I smiled, ignoring the stares from surrounding tables, and concentrated on my stuffed cabbage while my dinner companions gridlocked.

A plump middle-aged male customer walked by holding his plate piled high with buffet food. He almost dropped it on the floor when he saw two dykes in a tongue-kissing smooch. The waitresses, once they got an eyeful, huddled near the walls in semi-shock, looking scared.

It wasn't easy to get a refill on my decaf, let me tell you.

"But didn't you feel awkward or left out?" asked a friend when I was telling her about this later. Actually, no, I didn't. I understand the dizzy intoxication of dyke-love, and I love to see women kissing in public. Plus, Michèle and Anja did make an effort to talk with me each time they came up for air.

During one of these interludes, Anja, flushed, asked me, "It's okay with you, this? That we make such a reunion in the restaurant?"

"Oh, sure," I said, shrugging.

I recalled a previous dinner at the Staropolska, having an argument with an ex-lover. At one point she'd said she was upset about my new lover. "Why?" I'd asked dully, since, after all, she'd been the one to have a new lover first.

"Just because..." she said through clenched teeth and then shrieked loud enough for the people in surrounding booths to hear: "I CAN'T STOP THINKING ABOUT HOW THAT WOMAN IS PUTTING HER FINGER IN YOUR VAGINA!"

That had also caused a bit of a ripple at the old Staropolska.

On another occasion I'd met a male friend of mine there. He was going through a difficult time—and he cried pitifully, clasping my hand, all through dinner. The waitresses took turns passing our booth with eyebrows knit, as if to signal me that they were poised to call 911 at the slightest provocation.

"Don't worry," I said to Anja. "They know me here."

Still, this Dyke Kiss-In thing might have been a bit much for the Staropolskans. As Michèle and Anja and I were leaving, the cashier—who looks like a young Morticia Addams and, by the way, has a pretty butch haircut herself—scowled at me.

She's never done that before. Not even after the finger-in-the-vagina episode.

Despite the stares, Anja had enjoyed Staropolska. "Good sauerkraut, yum," she announced to all, patting her stomach, as we made our gracious exit.

"I like that place, Jorjet," said Michèle, zipping up her leather jacket against the January cold. "We'll have to come back here again sometime."

Quest for the Ancient Lesbonauts

Today Lesbomania travels back through the mists of time and space to explore one of the most profound question marks of herstory:

Has the Earth been visited by ancient lesbonauts from outer space? Is it true that thousands—perhaps even millions—of years ago, our Earth was first discovered by beautiful planet-leaping lesbians who were on an exploratory mission into deep space?

Lesbomania presents the evidence. You can decide for yourself.

First of all, the universe is now known to be largely empty, always expanding, and shaped, so scientists say, like a "donut."

With us on the inside.

A giant hollow donut?

What these scientists are really describing is a universe shaped like a huge, expanding vagina that folds back into itself to infinity!

Obviously scientists are not going to put the "V" word into the kiddie stargazing books. So we get donuts instead—consumer culture, and male symbolism, something with nuts in it.

But what are the ramifications of a universe that is actually a giant vagina?

It strongly suggests that ours is a universe that is highly favorable to the natural affinities of lesbians. And if there were more advanced, highly evolved lesbians eons ago, it would be perfectly natural that they would be "out" in space, happily probing the infinite foldings of our "donut"-shaped universe and our own Milky Way Galaxy.

Second point: A well-known scientist—you've probably seen him on television—has theorized that the reason myths from a number of different human cultures contain references to large beasts like "dragons" is because deep in our brains we *remember* beasts like dragons. That is, as mammals, we evolved from reptiles during the Triassic Age about 200 million years ago. And—according to this theory—our brain stems may still retain some kind of "shadow memory" of our dinosaur origins that then expressed itself in our human mythologies as "dragons."

But if this "shadow memory" concept is true, then Lesbomania must pose the obvious question:

Why is it that among lesbians there is such an emphasis on the idea of "space"?

Lesbians are always talking about "taking our space," "women's space," "lesbian space," "safe space," etc.

Space is obviously an integral part of the lesbian cosmological view.

Could it be that we lesbians did not evolve here on Earth from some now-extinct cold-blooded lizards, but in fact that this preoccupation with "space" is a brain stem "shadow memory" of our ancient origins on another planet?

A *lesbian planet* somewhere up there in outer...space?!

Seen in this light, it becomes clear why the male-dominated scientific establishment is so skeptical about the very existence of extraterrestrial life: These guys can't even see any lesbians on the Earth, so why would they recognize us in outer space?

They would sooner imagine monsters or little green men or giant humming rectangles than happy, well adjusted (and—

not incidentally—technologically superior) lesbians.

Scientists do concede the fact that the primordial life form is one sex, not two: female.

Couldn't it be, then, that the primordial female life form is the natural order in our vagina-shaped universe? And that life on other planets retains this all-female type of existence?

And that on our planet, something got screwed up?

For example, maybe some poor little protozoan back in the Pre-Cambrian era ingested some tiny piece of a crooked amino acid chain that was left floating in the chemical detritus of the Primordial Soup, and that garbage molecule she ate accidentally knocked an arm off one of her little x chromosomes...?

And boom! It was the world's first sex change!

This is not as improbable as you might imagine.

So far, our speculation has been highly theoretical.

Yet evidence is now mounting from prehistory and historical times that some of these lesbians from space have actually visited Earth and even possibly settled here!

Consider first the triangle. This modern symbol of gay and lesbian rights is actually a very ancient sign. In the Paleolithic or Old Stone Age, it was the primary symbol of the Goddess, graphically representing the female genital triangle. And zig-zag lines were sometimes drawn in conjunction with the triangle. According to archaelogist Marija Gimbutas, these zig-zag lines signified water, thereby conveying the pictographic message that the Goddess's vulva is the place from which precious moisture comes.

Now who would be most likely to invent a cosmology based on the sacredness of a wet vulva?

Who but...

...prehistoric lesbians!

Consider also that for thousands of years, over a wide geographical range, humans produced goddess statuary of all kinds. One of the major and earliest forms was a bird goddess. This image could be based on the actual experience of prehistoric humans who saw alien lesbians landing in their space ships!

Naturally, at the time, these lesbonauts would have seemed like goddesses to them.

Now let's consider the pyramids of Ancient Egypt. These architectural wonders and the secrets they hold have been the subject of speculation for 5,000 years.

The pyramids are made up of triangles—remember, that's the ancient symbol of the goddess's crotch—set to touch each other on their edges, turned with the bottom point up.

In other words, the pyramids are actually *giant three-dimensional vulvas aimed at outer space!*

Did ancient lesbonauts visiting Earth inspire this design and supervise the construction of these mysterious monuments?

The answer to this question is still unknown. But further investigation may prove that the pyramids were used as some kind of vibrational homing devices for the lesbian space travellers.

Even the Bible contains veiled references to visiting lesbonauts. For example, Luke 17:35 says: "Two women shall be grinding together, and the one shall be gone, while the other shall remain."

This passage could well be alluding to an affair between a

lesbonaut and a terrestrial lesbian, in which one must stay on Earth while her lover reluctantly must return to her hot lesbian home planet.

And in ancient Vulvanian—a lost language which was spoken in an area rich with prehistoric goddess statuary—an expression has survived that seems to be describing ancient lesbonauts:

Ugati....aliti....tiki....alura

which some paleolinguists have translated as: "Women who come...from the sky...and go down...on each other."

Bear in mind that our galaxy alone contains over 100 billion suns with countless planets capable of supporting life.

And where there's life, there are lesbians.

Therefore it's most probable that there are many *many* extraterrestrial lesbians.

So take heart. Whenever we look up at that glittery night sky, we are looking at a myriad of lesbian planets—filled with lesbians who are rooting for us down here on Earth.

My theory is just as good a theory as any other. It's no less probable than anybody else's. And until it's been proven otherwise, it's just as likely as any other to be true.

41

Gertie You're So Wordy!

This week marks the one-hundred-eighteenth birthday of lesbian literary lioness Gertrude Stein, born Feb. 3, 1874.

Even people who've never read a word of Stein's work have heard of That Couple: Gertrude Stein and Alice B. Toklas. Theirs was an old-fashioned, extreme kind of butch-femme domestic bliss, rarely seen today except among heterosexuals.

Picture it: In the evenings, a lovely dinner presided over by meticulous housewife Alice, topped off by some power-packed hashish brownies—Alice's special recipe—to release the creative juices. Then husband Gertrude, juices flowing, would retire to the study to write.

Gertie would fill page after page by hand, sometimes with only a few words on each sheet, chuckling to herself. The following morning bright and early, Alice would take these pages of handwritten gems her beloved had written the night before and type them up for posterity, often moved to shake her head in wonder at the brilliance of Gertrude's literary talent.

God bless Alice. Cook, housekeeper, typist, muse, cheerleader—the Compleat Femme.

Reading Stein (a sometimes disorienting experience without benefit of brownies), I was inspired to write the following tribute (it roughly goes to the tune of the classic rock and roll instrumental *Wipe Out*):

Ode to Gertrude

Everybody knows that a rose is a rose
is a rose is a rose is a rose.
But no one really *knows* why a rose is a rose
is a rose is a rose is a rose.

Ah, Gertie, you're a red hot mama!
Your paragraphs are pithy and dense
You hardly ever use a comma
But are your sentences supposed to *make sense*??

You say: "Pigeons on the grass, alas!" Alas! Alas!
Pigeons on the grass, alas?
You say: "A bay of say may Tuesday."
A bay of say may Tuesday?

Ah, Gertie, you're so wordy!
I love the way you use the present tense
Your paragraphs are down and dirty
But are your sentences supposed to *make sense*??

You know you never could have done it without Alice
She cooked and cleaned and took out the trash
While *you* wrote *her* "autobiography"
Alice baked your brownies 'n' hash!

Everybody cultivated Gertie
Matisse and Braque and the Fitzgeralds came to call
Picasso proclaimed her a "phenomenon!"
And Hemingway said, "She's got balls!"

Some people didn't think that Gertie Did It
That she and Alice were just dear devoted friends
But the Mystery still grows; not even JoAnn Loulan
        knows:
What *is* the sex life of a *perfect* butch and femme?

Oh, Gertie, you must've been a genius
Far ahead of your time without a doubt
'Cause it's more than half a century later
And they still can't figure you out!

Happy Birthday Gertie !

The Valentine Grinch

Love. Bah humbug.

Yes, yes, I know, it's Valentine's Day. For all of you who are in the throes of lesbian romantic bliss—the so-called Lesbian Insanity Period (or "LIP") at the beginning of a relationship—that must be very nice for you.

And also nice for you longtime lovers who are still sending each other sweets and leaving little bright red and white fluffy things around the house for each other to find. Like my dog Weasel who used to pick used tampons out of the garbage, chew them awhile, and present them back to us as tokens of her affection.

To all this Valentiny behavior I say bah humbug because, you see, I have HAD IT with love.

For awhile, anyway.

I need a rest. Last year was a really awful year for me emotionally. The pits. I'm still recuperating. The romantic parts were wonderful, as a matter of fact—but the breaking up stuff was hideous.

And don't kid yourselves, you newly-in-love lesbians; nine times out of ten you don't get one without the other, eventually.

So I decided that since I was still so fucked up from last year I was not, under any circumstances, going to fall in love during the next year, maybe two. No matter what incredible lesbians may show up in my life, if Cupid tries to shoot me with his arrow, I swear I'll wallop him over his curly little head with a giant electric Oster rechargeable Stick Massager.

Last year my astrologer gave me a full reading of my chart.

44

"Face it," she said. "You are a hopeless romantic."

Oh great.

"You've got an idealism having to do with sexual relationships...."

Me and every other dyke over thirty-five, I thought.

"You have deep, intense emotions, and pleasure is more important to you than discipline."

Truer words were never spoken. Well, this astrologer also knows me pretty well, whatever the stars say. She's not an ex of mine, but she's an ex of one of my exes.

Then, after Chicago's annual Capricorn Party last month (Chicago lesbian Capricorns are notoriously well-organized, just as one would expect), a few of my friends were sitting around talking about our New Year's resolutions.

"Mine is: I'm not going to fall in love this year," I announced.

This was greeted by general laughter: "Ho ho, you can't stop yourself from falling in love!"

"Why not?" I said, a bit miffed.

"You're such a passionate person. You really think you can give up sex for a whole year?"

"Who said anything about giving up *sex?*" I said. "I'm not saying I'm not up for some fooling around. Quite the opposite, if it's light and fun and friendly. But LOVE?—forget it."

More laughter. It was pointed out to me that I do have a tendency to fall in love with the women I sleep with.

"Not this year," I insisted. "But if it comes down to no sex either, so be it. Nothing is worth what I went through last year. At least my vibrator isn't going to break my heart. My vibrator isn't going to scream at me in public places. My vibrator isn't going to leave drunken abusive calls on my answering machine. Or...."

"I bet you will too fall in love this year," one friend said. "I'll bet five bucks that you do."

Luckily, another friend of mine, somebody who's known me for years, came to my rescue and took her up on the bet.

"Whew," I said, "Thanks. It's good to know that *somebody* believes I have the fortitude to make it an entire year without going gaga."

"Well, what the heck, it's only five bucks on the line here," she reminded me.

An old and dear friend, a straight woman who lives in Pennsylvania now, told me on the phone that she was also willing to bet five bucks that I WON'T fall in love this year. "You can do it," she said earnestly. "I know you can."

The way she said it reminded me of a woman in a movie once who comforted an accident victim by assuring him he would walk again despite what the doctor said.

I ran back to my astrologer for a six-month update.

Not that I believe in astrology, you understand.

She said, "Uranus is trining your Venus, so you can avoid falling in love this year if you really want to. In fact, Uranus is the planet of (among other things) exciting one-night stands."

Wow. I told my friend who had bet I'd fall in love about this interesting astrological forecast. "That's not fair, checking your chart," she said. "That's like peeking."

Well, maybe so, but it made me feel better. Incurable romantic though I may be, I need a vacation from all the drama and fighting and heavy emotion and angst. I need some simple uncomplicated fun.

So, Cupid, shoot your dumb love arrows at somebody else for awhile. I can live without the cards and the candy and the cooing.

For one little old year, at least.

Even my astrologer says I can.

(Sniffle.)

I'm a Maniac, Maniac...

As a dyed-in-the-wool lesbomaniac, naturally I believe that if everyone else was one, too, the world would be a healthier place.

Now, medically speaking, there are plenty of other manias already, and some of them are a drag. Like kleptomania, the compulsion to steal.

Or pyromania, a need to set fires. Or dipsomania, a terrible craving for liquor.

Or how about siderodromomania, a compulsion for travelling by train? Who but an ink-blot tester would want symmetromania, a mania for symmetry? Or the serious medical problems of trichorrhexomania—a compulsion to pinch your hairs off?

But lots of manias are harmless or even positive. President Franklin Delano Roosevelt had timbromania, an obsession with postage stamps, and it didn't hurt him one bit—in fact he found it educational and inspirational. Hydromania, the need to be near water, might be just perfect for a sailor. And a professional dancer would probably benefit from a case of choreomania, a fanatic interest in dancing.

Roget's Thesaurus cites satyromania and andromania as two terms for obsessive lust in (for?) men. And for obsessive lust in women: there's the old standby, nymphomania, sure—but there's also hysteromania, oestromania, and uteromania.

Uteromania??

Also according to Roget, gymnomania is a preoccupation with nakedness, mentulomania is an obsession with penises ("mentula" is an archaic medical term for penis), and orchid-omania is a fanatic interest, not in orchids, but in testicles.

I think somebody Way Back When must have had a mania for making up manias.

Roget's Fourth Edition lists them all. I looked them up because I have a touch of logomania when it comes to words.

Anyway, not surprisingly, lesbomania isn't on the list yet. But lately I've seen the term used in a few other gay and lesbian publications. It's only a matter of time before the term gets picked up by the world at large.

Because lesbomania is a concept whose time has definitely come.

And being a lesbomaniac is an entirely positive, intense, and euphoric experience.

Don't just take my word for it. Ask any lesbomaniac—she'll tell you the same thing.

Otherwise she wouldn't be one. By definition.

Give Me An L!

As far as I know, I invented the word "lesbomania."

It came to me in a flash, as I was trying to think up a snappy name for my column.

At the time, a lot of columnists were using the word "Out" in the title of their columns in one way or another, so that was, um, out. And I wanted the title to have some specific reference to lesbians.

"Lesboland"—as someone suggested to me—seemed a bit silly.

"Lesboteque" seemed impossibly dated.

"Lesbotica" sounded like a cross between erotica and robotics.

"Dykes-R-Us" was just too cutesy.

"Clits 'N' Tits" was a little too crass.

So, since I can be downright cheerleaderlike on the subject of lesbians, Lesbomania seemed to sum it up.

Briefly, I toyed with the idea of spelling it "Lesbomynia," to avoid offending separatist womyn who don't like having a "man" in anything. But that seemed too complicated, and anyway it would sound different.

And mania, not mynia, is an important part of the idea.

If you saw the word "lesbomania" in print anywhere before you saw it in my column, I'd be interested in knowing where. I do want to give credit where credit is due, and I suppose it's possible that somebody else invented it first and I innocently dredged it up out of my unconscious, the way George Harrison claimed he got the tune for *My Sweet Lord* out of *He's So Fine*.

But barring evidence to the contrary, I claim "lesbomania"

as my very own brainchild. I want credit for having coined the term. I want my name right there as the originator of "lesbomania" listed in the word origin books of the twenty-first century.

Because, mark my words, lesbomania is someday going to be a phenomenon—like Beatlemania or disco-mania.

I don't mean that my column is going to be a phenomenon—I don't have any grandiose visions about that, believe me.

I mean lesbomania itself. Like any enthusiast, I naturally want the thing that interests me most and excites me most to become popularized. I want to see it sweeping the land! I want it to be the topic on everyone's lips!

If we could have the twist and hula hoops and disco-fever and wave after wave of other trendy pop fevers, why not lesbo-fever?

Surely some young dyke out there could invent a lesbian dance to kick off the craze?

Instead of working-class John Travolta hoofing robustly in *Saturday Night Fever*, trying with every fiber of his being to win the coveted prize in the dance contest, as the Bee Gees wail *Stayin' Alive, Stayin' Alive* in the background, how about a movie all about working-class lesbians dancing robustly in their local community bar, competing to win the coveted prize in the dance contest, with, say, the Dyketones wailing *Stayin' a Dyke, Stayin' a Dyke* in the background?

Well, it would be a little schlocky, but I managed to sit through that Travolta movie when it came out, so you know I would have been thrilled to sit through a dyke flick with the same plot.

Imagine how much further along in the fight against homophobia we'd be now if, back then, we'd had whole audiences humming along, snapping their fingers, rooting for that slick-haired butch and her feisty femme to win the dance contest despite all odds: *Stayin' a Dyke, Stayin' a Dyke...*

And I think the lesbian cheerleader idea has great potential.

Picture Olivia Newton-John in her felt skirt and pom poms,

leaping and bounding in the school gym for the lesbian softball team. Just like in *Grease*, but it's:

Give me an L! Give me an E!...

Wish I'd had the chance to do that when I was in high school. Maybe Olivia does, too.

C'mon Olivia, let's all give it a try together.

Here we go—

Give me an L! Give me an E!...

Elizabethan Drama

I don't have a neon pink triangle or a purple labrys hanging in the window of my apartment, but it must be pretty clear to the neighbors that I'm not a single gal in search of a husband. My lover drives a huge red convertible which no one on the block has failed to notice, and dykey-looking women wearing *Outlines* T-shirts are always ringing my doorbell.

My neighborhood is not the hippest, and it sure ain't Chicago's "gay ghetto," Newtown. But Mountain Moving Coffeehouse, the oldest ongoing women-only gathering space in the world, used to hold its events at a rented space in a church right around the corner. So it was kind of fun to watch the expressions of puzzlement on our straight neighbors' faces when droves of dykes converged on the area every Saturday night.

My western windows face a single-family house owned by a genuine nuclear family—husband, wife, and four kids. They have vicious arguments. Their yelling—and sometimes the screams and crying of the children—can be heard way out into the street. The cops have been called many times.

Needless to say, they are not ideal neighbors, especially when I need to get some sleep and they are re-enacting the Battle of Gallipoli in their bedroom.

Benny, the third child of this unhappy family, is about seven. Usually a very quiet kid, he was bouncing a volleyball in front of our building one sunny Saturday afternoon this spring while my friend and upstairs neighbor, Paula, was sitting on our porch steps.

"You don't go to the *Elizabeth* Church, do you?" he asked her.

"The what?" said Paula.

"The Elizabeth Church. You know, where all the Elizabeths go."

Then, of course, Paula understood. She and I and our lovers sometimes walked to Mountain Moving Coffeehouse together on a Saturday evening.

Paula, amused, asked him, "What's an Elizabeth?"

Benny, still bouncing his volleyball, said, "That's when two girls kiss each other *all the time.*"

He made an ugly face to demonstrate his revulsion.

"That doesn't sound so bad to me," Paula replied.

"Oh, it is," he told her, shaking his head. "It's really *bad.*"

The windows of Paula's apartment, like mine, face Benny's parents' house, and she, too, has heard the shouts from their war zone.

"You know what I think is bad?" Paula said to the boy. "When people yell and scream and act mean to each other."

This caught Benny by surprise. He didn't have a ready answer. He stopped bouncing his ball and stood there thinking.

"Yes," he said pensively. "That's not good at all."

"And I think kissing is a lot better than that," Paula added.

He stood there awhile longer, the volleyball still frozen in his hands. Finally he said, "Yes, you're *right.*" Then, quick as a flash, he ran off down the street.

Ever since this talk, Benny has been very nice to us Elizabeths—and his mother has been friendlier. Probably it's a coincidence, but maybe Benny said something at home that was able to make a difference—because since then the loud, terrible arguments have significantly diminished, too.

Jesse Helms and the Coalition for Family Values, take note. Here's a clear case in which a lesbian has undermined the nuclear family—undermined its child abuse, domestic violence, and homophobia.

Dammit, Janet!

Finally it's springtime. And, so the poem goes: "In the spring, the young dyke's fancy lightly turns to thoughts of love..."

Okay—so I'm paraphrasing just a little. I don't think Alfred Lord Tennyson would have minded the lesbian lyric change. And if so, so what?

Spring has traditionally been a time for poetry and song—maybe because it sets the hormones a-humming. But the ideal of Springtime Love is no longer just bucolic countryside and birds and bees and Girl Meets Girl. Here in the complicated Gay Nineties, it's more like Walden Pond meets Beaver Dam.

So I wrote an Ode to Springtime that finally acknowledges one of the major quandaries of Modern Lesbian Romance—you can sing it (with hormones humming along, if you like) to the tune of the 1950s skiffle music classic, *Does Your Chewing Gum Lose Its Flavor on the Bedpost Overnight?*

So strike up that banjo in the key of D-major! And a-one, and a-two, and a-three, and a-four:

> Oh me oh my oh you—
> Whatever shall I do?
> Hallelujah, the problem is peculiah
> I'd give a lot of dough
> If only I could know
> The answer to my question,
> Is it yes or is it no?

CHORUS:
Does your dental dam lose its flavor
On the bedpost overnight?
If your lover says don't chew on it
Do you swallow it in spite?
Can you catch it on your tonsils?
Can you heave it left and right?
Does your dental dam lose its flavor
On the bedpost overnight?

FIRST VERSE:
She went to Paris Dance
In search of some romance
Soon she was swimmin'
In a dancing sea of wimmin
Then she became aware
The crowd had stopped to stare—
As the drunken voice of her ex-lover
Thundered through the air— Shouting:

> (Chorus) "Does your dental dam lose its flavor
> On the bedpost overnight...?" etc.

SECOND VERSE:
It was at a press conference
For a closeted actress
They asked about her figure
And her upcoming picture
There was lots of repartee
About her fiance—
Then someone piped up from the back
And said, "Oh, by the way—

> (Chorus) Does your dental dam lose its flavor
> On the bedpost overnight?
> If you soak it for a day in a glass of Perrier
> Then will it taste all right?..." etc.

THIRD VERSE:
She was in the dentist's chair
For major orthodontic care
The dentist was so lovely
Her face so warm and bubbly
That that poor patient, she
Was hoping there might be
    A double meaning in the
    Sexy dentist's inquiry:

    (Chorus) Does your dental dam lose its flavor
    On the bedpost overnight?

LAST VERSE:
She tried so many stores
Walgreens, Osco, and Phar-Mors
The pharmacists weren't shocked
But dams they never stocked
Puzzled by her request
Their ignorance they confessed:
Why would anyone need a dental dam
At a women's music fest?

(Final Chorus) Does your dental dam lose its flavor
On the bedpost overnight?

Bad Attitude

I'm on my way to Atlanta, Georgia, for a truly historic, whoops, herstoric event: the National Lesbian Conference.

Picture it: Fragrant magnolia trees sway in the balmy southern spring breezes. Lesbian visibility all over the place. Lesbian energy. Lesbian culture. Lesbian lesbians.

So why do I feel like I'm on the way to the dentist's office for major bridgework? Like this is something I have to do because, despite the pain and discomfort, ultimately it will be good for me?

I know that hundreds and hundreds of women have worked countless hours to bring the Lesbian Agenda—as the pre-conference organizing workers have called the project—to fruition. I also know that the path to this conference is strewn with the wreckage of bitter, burned-out organizers, disgusted ex-fundraisers, and ex-volunteers who feel they have been through the wringer.

To put it more politely: Turnover among the pre-conference organizers has been high.

Now, a National Lesbian Conference doesn't happen every day, and this promises to be a precedent-setting, historic, whoops, herstoric event. Yet hardly anybody I know in Chicago is going. Those who haven't been through the cuisinart in the planning stages have been put off by the horror stories of women desperately clutching crystals for guidance during organizational meetings.

I love to spend time thinking about lesbians and who we are and what we are doing. But worrying about "political correctness" has never been my concern. Not that I've ever been accused of being politically incorrect, particularly.

Always a first time, though, eh? And this may be it.

The whole idea of "political correctness" has seemed so Orwellian to me that sometimes I think that to be politically incorrect is more politically correct than being politically correct.

If you get my drift.

An ex-lover of mine once bragged to her friends (we were still lovers at the time) that I was "*instinctively* politically correct."

I took this, well, not as a complete compliment, but as a kind of—what do they call it in the Catholic Church?— *absolution*. PC/PI-free (i.e., sin-free like the Virgin Mary), I could sail through life with a minimum of "processing."

I get processed enough by mainstream culture to turn my brain to cheese dip already.

So at first I decided not to go to the conference, if it meant I was in for a giant dose of political correctitude. I'd heard plenty about that from ex-organizers already.

Then I reconsidered. There will be lesbians from all over the country! What an opportunity it will be to talk about our many diverse visions of Lesbian Nation!

So I bought my ticket. And I went to Woolworth's and bought some politically correct fragrance-free deodorant for the trip. And I began studying the conference literature.

I glanced at an NLC newsletter and read: "The NLC continues to be a learning coalition effort. In that spirit, we note that there is an ongoing debate within the visually impaired community about whether the use of the word 'vision' is sightist or not. We apologize for anyone we have offended by using it and recognize the need to be sensitive to our use of language."

Gak! Guilty of being politically incorrect! And if the word "vision" has to go out the window, I guess I'd better think twice about promoting "lesbian *visibility*," hadn't I? Clearly I need to attend the intensive "anti-oppression" sessions scheduled all over the conference agenda.

I admit I have a bad attitude. I'm suspicious that "anti-oppression work" means long, grueling confrontations in which lesbians try to convince each other that "I'm more oppressed than you are." But I'd better go, and take my medicine like a big girl.

Uh-oh. Did I say something sizeist?

Yes, the Lesbian Conference promises to be a learning experience, if nothing else.

Maybe at least there'll be some fun, old-fashioned lesbian pajama parties in the hotel.

Unless some lesbian is offended by pajamas...?

...Or by parties...?

...Or by fun...?

...Or by lesbians...?

Beyond the Fringe

I dreaded going to the National Lesbian Conference in Atlanta.

Not because I was worried about lesbian-hating bigots storming the hotel hosting the conference, or worried about fundamentalist homophobes bombing the plenary sessions at the Atlanta Civic Center. Such thoughts never even crossed my paranoid little mind.

No. I was afraid that the NLC was going to be so dominated by fringe groups dumping on each other that the conference would be a fiasco. That the internecine lesbian warfare would be so awful it might actually turn me off to lesbian culture altogether.

Which would be pretty bad, considering that I'm a lesbo-maniac.

Well, I went. And honestly, I had a fantastic time. Those NLC organizing gals (whoever they were—some women spent a good deal of the weekend trying to find out who was running things), they really knew how to put on a show.

Not that shit didn't happen. A *lot* of shit happened. But so much of it was fascinating—even if it was in a surreal way.

Admittedly, I had been prepared for the worst. As women stepped up to microphones at a pre-plenary session to scream unfulfillable demands and accuse each other of being oppressive, I calmly sat reading my shelf-worn copy of *The Gentle Art of Verbal Self Defense.*

I turned to a friend sitting next to me after one lesbian delivered a particularly angry, abusive rant about how some previous speaker had oppressed her by their use of the insulting phrase "dominant culture" when referring to rich, white, straight men.

Incidentally, this was supposed to be a session to discuss a future national Lesbian political organization.

"Hey, cheer up," I said, noticing that my friend was holding her head in her hands. "This isn't nearly as bad as I expected."

She shot me a pained expression. Right in front of my eyes I could see her dream of Lesbian Nation congealing into a migraine headache.

"Then you must have been expecting World War Three," she said.

Sure, there were moments of despair. Like when the Lesbians in the Military almost got in a fist fight in the aisle with Lesbians Against the War, for instance.

But there were so many high points that counterbalanced the lows.

Like the eighteen naked Amazons who quietly snuck into the Radisson Hotel's swimming pool for an illegal midnight swim and lesbian love-in after a particularly chaotic plenary session.

Like the lesbian who, during a memorial for lesbian loved ones who have died, insisted on including "all the lesbian dogs who have been tortured to death in laboratory experiments."

Like the 400-pound woman in the anti-fat-oppression workshop who stood up and pulled down her pants, and proudly demonstrated how her stomach is an erogenous zone, exclaiming: "My belly hangs over my pussy!"

Like the jovial group of lesbians of color at the Atlanta airport Sunday night, waiting for their plane back to New York, who were able to keep a positive attitude while recounting all the conference's disasters. "I'm going to make up T-shirts for all of us," one woman said to the rest of the group, "that will say: 'I Survived the National Lesbian Conference.' "

She's right. We survived.

And we'll keep on surviving. My faith in lesbians was renewed at the NLC conference because I came to the conclusion that no matter how we bicker among ourselves and

61

cause each other grief, lesbians are without a doubt the most interesting group of people on this planet.

But then, I may be a little biased. Considering that I am, after all, a lesbomaniac.

Presto Change-O!

According to ancient Greek mythology, Medusa—one of three supposedly hideous monsters called the Gorgons—was so terrible to look at that glancing at her face would instantly turn a person to stone. In another Greek tale of transformation, everything touched by King Midas turned instantly into gold. (Unfortunately for him, this included his food and his family.)

The Christian tradition also abounds with tales of instant transformation, including Paul's conversion on the road to Damascus, and the modern-day "born again" phenomenon.

And now, according to some homophobes in the city of Chicago, apparently glancing at a picture of two men or two women kissing is going to instantly turn straight people queer.

If only it were true.

I'm referring to the New York arts collective Gran Fury's poster which now, despite bitter opposition, can be seen on the sides of a few city buses and at a few Chicago Transit Authority locations. This poster shows three couples who are kissing—one straight, one gay male, one lesbian.

That seems pretty democratic to me. But critics of the poster have said it "promotes" homosexuality. Columnist Mike Royko had one of his increasingly frequent anti-gay hissy fits over it. And Alderman Robert Shaw thinks it will "convert viewers to homosexuality."

While homophobes register their indignation, so far, preliminary reports of miracle "conversions" have been highly encouraging:

• Last week rush-hour crowds were startled when a young man glanced at the poster on the Ravenswood el station, and immediately ran off to catch the bus to North Halsted Street, shouting "I'm one!"

• A distraught high school principal reported that after a bus displaying the poster drove by his school, an entire girls' gym class was caught making out in the showers.

• A commodities broker who was out walking his dog past the poster returned home to discover his Brooks Brothers three-piece suit had turned into a neon ensemble from Bad Boys, and his pit bull was now an afghan.

• Two skinhead queerbashers who saw the poster reported that their boxer shorts turned into Calvin Klein underwear, and their hair had grown out into a shelf-cut. Their boom box, which had been playing Guns n' Roses, suddenly began Act Two of *Aida*, although they had not touched the tuner. Sheepishly, they admitted they were attracted to each other.

• At a Daughters of the American Revolution luncheon, several of the ladies were discovered to have inexplicably acquired shoulder tattoos. Later they recalled that their limousine had driven past a CTA bus displaying the "love" poster.

• Two men reported missing on their way to a Bears game were found signing up for the bridal registry at Marshall Fields.

• At a West Side wedding ceremony, the bride threw herself into the arms of the maid of honor, the groom embraced the best man, and both couples demanded a double wedding on the spot.

• As a postered bus passed a Protestant church, the choir abruptly segued from "A Mighty Fortress Is Our God" into the chorus of "Leaping Lesbians."

• The chairman of the Burroughs Wellcome corporation announced that he was joining ACT UP/Chicago.

The miracle poster is also reported to have acted as a strong suppressant on many homophobes, who, upon viewing it, shrunk back, melted, and vanished.

Both Robert Shaw and Mike Royko have mysteriously turned to stone. Negotiations are underway for their lifelike statues to be put on permanent display at the Chicago Historical Society.

And, perhaps the juiciest item of all, anti-gay fanatic Anita Bryant, after receiving a copy of the poster from an outraged fundamentalist, has turned into a pillar of salt.

Poetic justice.

All of which only goes to show what we knew all along: In America, it pays to advertise.

Fest Side Story

I've been working on my lesbian musical, an all-woman version of *West Side Story*. It's a tragic tale of star-crossed love between an idealistic young ultra-radical lesbian separatist and a freewheeling apolitical devil-may-care girljock of polymorphous sexual persuasion.

Each belongs to her own gang of friends. And the feuding between the two hostile subculture gangs—instead of the Jets and the Sharks, here it's the Seps and the Tarts—sets off a chain of events in which the innocent young lovers are doomed.

It begins as Richi and Natalie meet by accident at a late-night dance at a women's music festival.

They are enchanted by each other—it's as if the rest of the dance tent had dissolved away, and only the two of them exist.

In a rousing song, the nervous Seps warn Richi against Natalie, since she's a Tart and may even be bisexual. She can't be a *real* lesbian, they sing, because *When you're a dyke you're a dyke all the way, you are never a het, there is no fuckin' way....*

The Tarts, led by Natalie's overly protective sister George and George's lover Rita, tell the naive Natalie that the Seps have made them feel like second-class lesbians simply because of their laissez-faire approach to sex. They sing and dance lustily: *I like to be in a merry cunt, okay by me in a merry cunt....*

Can the young lovers overcome the hatred of the two warring groups? In a momentary burst of hope, they think of one thing they all can agree on despite their vast cultural differ-

66

ences, and they sweetly sing as a duet:

> The most beautiful sound I ever heard:
> Martina—Martina Martina Martina!
> All the beautiful sounds of the world in a single word:
> Martina—Martina, Martina Martina!
> Martina Martina Martina—
> Mar-TEE-na! I've just seen a dyke named Martina,
> And suddenly that name will never be the same for
>   me.
> Martina, I've just watched a game with Martina,
> And suddenly I've found
> How wonderful a sound can be!
> Martina, say it loud and it's tennis playing,
> Say it soft and it's tennis skirts swaying.
> Martina, I'll never stop saying Martina!

(Here, the instrumental bridge comes in with violins and added tennis ball thwumping sounds, during which Richi and Natalie, holding hands, gaze off beyond their squalid, hastily-erected tents toward an immaculate tennis court hovering in a cloudless blue sky.)

> Martina! Say it loud, it's a dyke sensation.
> Say it soft, and it's Lesbian Nation.
> Martina, I'll never stop saying Martina...!

The young lovers vow that if they can't reconcile their gangs, the two of them will run away and seek work together at a tennis camp (and here they sing the plaintive *There's a Space for us, somewhere a Space for us...*).

But the subcultures' hostility proves too powerful for them when the Seps and the Tarts rumble in the chem-free camping area. In the melee, Richi's best friend Russ and Natalie's sister George are fatally wounded. Rita becomes crazed with thoughts of vengeance. Richi, who at Russ's demise is thrust into the position of Leader of the Seps, is chased by angry Tarts into a portajane.

Natalie rushes in to save her.

Too late—for the portajane topples over, smothering the lovers and burying forever their dream of lesbonuptial bliss.

Humbled and united at last by this senseless tragedy, the Seps and Tarts vow that from now on they will stop sniping at each other in lesbian publications, and learn to live in the peace and harmony for which the young lovers have paid such a terrible price at the music festival.

Curtain.

The Ghost of Christmas Past

Scene: A picturesque little Presbyterian church on a side street in ye olde New York City borough of Queens.

Time: December 1960, a more innocent era, back when gangs jumped people but rarely shot them, and the drug of choice was not crack cocaine but hobby airplane glue inhaled from a paper bag.

In the church hall, my young adult Sunday School class—ten wiseass, punky white kids age thirteen—slouched towards Bethlehem around a wooden table as we discussed the meaning of the Nativity.

Our teacher, Mr. Toschke, was a timid, kindly, devout grey-haired gentleman who had no control whatsoever over the foul-mouthed juvenile delinquents he'd been saddled with in the name of religious education.

We amused ourselves by trying to torture and embarrass him as much as possible.

Mr. Toschke read out loud how the Angel Gabriel came down unto Mary to tell her that God had singled her out as Blessed Among Women. The Angel Gabriel whispered into Mary's ear, and she became filled with the Holy Spirit.

At that moment, said Mr. Toschke, Our Savior was conceived.

"You saying she got pregnant through her ear?" said Alice Brown from under a thick crust of pancake makeup, black mascara, and white lipstick.

She popped her bubblegum thoughtfully. "Holy Cow."

Someone else asked: "But how did God's sperm get into the Angel Gabriel's mouth?"

"Oh, gross!" We all squealed and pounded the table.

Poor Mr. Toschke tried to ignore our blasphemy and plowed on. "God sent Jesus because He loveth all His children, all races, all colors, all creeds."

Bobby Harmintz, one of the major class troublemakers, piped up: "But God must love women better than men."

"What?" said Mr. Toschke.

"Sure," Bobby snorted. "Otherwise, God would be *queer*."

Nowadays, more sexually-attuned thirteen-year-olds might respond with a shrug: "Maybe God's bi." Some really awake kid might even ask, "Why is God always portrayed as male, anyway?"

But back then, a shocked silence fell over our young adult class.

Bobby Harmintz had gone too far.

Even kids who had no idea what it meant knew that "queer" was on the roster of curse words.

In retrospect, I think Bobby Harmintz was gay-baiting Mr. Toschke, a rather feminine man who described himself as a lifelong "confirmed bachelor." But at the time, such matters went right over my head. I was not a lesbian-atheist-pagan back then, but a teenybopper-quasi-Presbyterian-wannabee, and I was concerned that a thunderbolt could whomp down to wipe out the entire young adult class as a result of Bobby's sacrilege.

I decided somebody had better come to God's defense.

"But...God had Jesus with Mary, so he couldn't have been...that," I said.

"Sure he could," said Bobby with an Elvis sneer, as if he knew a lot more about these things than I did. (And he did— as I gather from later reports.)

"But God was sort of married to Mary in a way, wasn't he?" I mused in my thirteen-year-old religious romance-comic haze. "I mean, he picked Mary out of all the other women to have his kid with."

Bobby snapped back impatiently, "No stupid, she *already* was married. To Joseph."

I covered my mouth with my hand. "Hey, that's right! But then, that means that God was committing adultery with somebody else's wife! That's against the Ten Commandments!"

And we all turned our gaze to the now crimson-faced Mr. Toschke for an answer to this conundrum.

At such moments—and there were many such moments in our young adult class—Mr. Toschke in his desperation retreated into an almost Catholic mysticism. He merely said, in a small, trembling Mr. Peepers voice, "The Lord works in mysterious ways."

Doesn't She, though?

Like Ebenezer Scrooge, one comes to see the past in a new light.

I'm sorry we teased Mr. Toschke so mercilessly. From my vantage point thirty-some-odd (some very odd) years later, I suppose our "confirmed bachelor" Sunday School teacher—now long dead—was, like God, probably Queer after all.

Merry Solstice!

Michiguilt

Goddess help me, but I'm not going to Michigan!

I've already been to one lesbian festival this summer and I'm going to another one Labor Day Weekend. Isn't that enough?!!

No!

Michigan is the Big Mama of festivals—the largest, most tradition-packed, the most mystique-filled.

Also the most uncomfortable, injury- and disease-prone, overwhelming, crowded...

But I *have* to go to Michigan!

But I *hate camping.*

Each year I go through this indecision, this Michig-angst, until my ambivalence reaches a fever pitch by the weekend before the festival.

I didn't go last year because I was sick: I got a migraine from trying to decide whether to go or not.

The year before, my ride fell through—lucky for me, since that was the year so many women there got violently ill from shigella.

But if I don't go this year, it will be the third year in a row that I haven't gone!

"I understand. It's okay," a friend consoles me. "I went through a period when I took a few years off, too."

Note the phrase: "Took a few years off." As if attending the festival is a necessary chore—or the sacred duty of every good lesbian.

Some women save their money for years and travel halfway around the world to come to the Michigan Festival. And I, who live in Chicago, a mere five hours away, am not going?

How can I be such an ingrate?

My Right Brain argues with my Left Brain: "Think of what she'll miss if she doesn't go! Days of productive networking, communing with nature, seeing all those wonderful women performers...."

My Left Brain argues back: "What about that year it constantly rained, her tent flooded, and she slept in a pool of muddy water for four days? She's nuts to go to Michigan unless she's in a Winnebago with full rations of food and water. Think of it: all those days in the woods, exposed to the elements. Eating nothing but fried tofu in yogurt sauce..."

"So what's a little discomfort when it comes to experiencing lesbian culture?" says my Right Brain. "Isn't lesbian culture worth a few bug bites?"

Michiguilt!

Okay, I'll go, I'll go.

"Sure," says my Left Brain. "And she can be a part of all that marvellous political *processing.*"

That's it. I'm not going.

Right Brain: "But it's Lesbian Nation! Beautiful Michigoddesses...."

Left Brain: "Mishuggenahs! Dust, heat, thunderstorms...."

Right Brain: "Seven thousand women! Many of them stark na...."

I'm going.

Last week, in the midst of this Michigaas, I ran into a very well-known Chicago lesbian activist, who asked me if I was going to the festival.

"I don't know," I groaned.

"I'm going," she said. "Finally." She leaned toward me, lowered her voice and said, "I've never been before. Shhh-h-h, don't tell anyone."

How many lesbians are walking around Chicago hiding this secret shame?

On the other hand, an editor at a New York gay and lesbian magazine who has no shame whatsoever calls me up to see if

I'll cover the festival for her paper. "What I want is a kind of anthropological approach," she says.

This editor has never been to the festival, has no interest in going, and may not have a clear idea of where the state of Michigan, never mind the festival, is located.

"I want something like '*National Geographic goes to Amazon Woodstock*,'" she tells me. "You can put in stuff about the history of the festival, too—oh, and don't forget to mention that year when everybody got trenchmouth."

"Shigella," I said weakly.

"Yeah, right. Whatever."

No. I'm not doing it. *I'm not even going.*

Can't I just stay home and relax? Maybe go to the Ferron concert or the Joan Armatrading concert, spend a day in bed with my girlfriend, take warm showers, read a Naiad novel....

But how can I resist Michigan's magnetic pull? The magic of all those lesbians gathered in one place? It's so tempting....

I keep reminding myself: I hate camping. I hate camping. *Oh how I hate camping.*

Goddess help me! I'm not going to Michigan!

Unless I change my mind tomorrow.

Space Invaders

"Veterans" of the Michigan Womyn's Music Festival come home and tell what we jokingly call "war stories" about the festival—the weather, the issues, the intrigues. But among this year's "war stories" is one that sounds almost like a bad World War I movie.

It seems that a small plane (with its registration number hidden) flew over the Main Stage area Saturday evening, making several passes, dropping pro-sadomasochist literature.

"Some women thought it was Jesus Freaks," said a friend of mine who saw the plane. "Most of the leaflets—I'd say about 90 percent—landed in the woods, so it was hard to even find a copy. And the few that didn't fall into the underbrush were wet from the rain."

The "leaflet" turned out to be S/M-related articles from two gay publications and a letter from S/M dykes in response to the festival's new S/M-restrictive policy.

I asked another lesbian who had been at the festival about the airplane caper.

"It wasn't S/M women," she said firmly. "It was the CIA."

"What makes you say that?"

"You know how much money it would cost to rent a plane to do that? And they didn't just drop leaflets out. That plane was using a sophisticated, expensive leaflet-ejecting machine—like the CIA would use."

"But why," I asked, "would the CIA fly over Michigan to

dump S/M literature?"

She gave me a 'you-are-very-naive' look. "To cause divisions in the community."

"Oh."

I can see the CIA agents now, poring over gay and lesbian publications, deciding what literature to dump. One agent says to the other, "Why don't we just put some more shigella in the food this year, and make them all sick?" The other replies, "No, heh-heh, this will be more *divisive*."

And here I had been imagining the most prominent advocate of lesbian S/M, Pat Califia, up there in that vibrating cockpit: Whack! "Dump those leaflets, you worthless slaves—hurry up, and I'll let you lick my boots!"

"Oh, thank you, mistress...."

I tell this CIA twist to another Michigan "veteran."

"What paranoid garbage," she says. "It couldn't have been the CIA. They're too incompetent. If it had been the CIA, they would have crashed the plane."

Tapping into my vast network of lesbian journalistic sources, I called yet another woman who was at the festival. She confirmed that it had been an S/M operation, and knew the names of the S/M dykes who had actually hired the pilot.

"Well," I said, "I hope at least it was a *female* pilot."

Silence.

"Hey!" I said. "I was just joking. You mean to tell me that...?"

"Um," she said, apologetically, "they couldn't find any women pilots in the area...."

Great Goddess! So it wasn't Pat Califia up there, nor some latter-day Amelia Earhart, for that matter. It was some *guy* pummeling unsuspecting dyke nudists with leather leaflets! No wonder he dropped them all into the woods—he was preoccupied: glued to his binoculars.

What now? Will next year's pie chart of festival expenses show a slice of money allocated for anti-aircraft and camouflage gear, right there next to the slices for land taxes and performer costs?

Sadomasochists, *How could you?*

Hiring a male to invade lesbian space?! "Cockpit" indeed!

In the ideological dogfight over S/M, this latest "man"-euver must surely be the unkindest cut (ouch) of all.

The 'Face on Mars' Comes Out

The mysterious mile-wide Face on Mars is trying to talk!

"The lips are trying to move, say stunned scientists," according to the *Weekly World News.*

Scientists may be stunned, but any lesbomaniac will conclude that this is just more proof that the universe is filled with extraterrestrial lesbians—and that they have been trying to contact us.

After all, isn't this one of the most lesbomaniacal things you've ever heard: *Giant mile-wide lips moving on another planet?*

The Face on Mars was discovered twenty years ago. So how come it's started talking now? Read on.

According to the *Weekly World News*, photos taken by the Soviet Mars Orbitter and transmitted back to Earth have produced "more questions than answers," says one scientist who is analyzing the pictures.

I'll bet.

You may recall earlier articles about this phenomenon. At first, the Face on Mars was identified as Elvis Presley. But as anyone can see, this giant stone face doesn't look anything like Elvis.

And who it *is* is as plain as the nose on its face: The Face on Mars is a giant replica of the face of Edie Sedgwick.

For those of you who may not know, Edie Sedgwick was a young East Coast heiress who dyed her hair white to look exactly like Andy Warhol and who was part of Warhol's entourage in the Sixties. She was frequently incoherent, somnambulistic, and always looked bored and generally miserable. Stony faced, you might say. She died stoned, too, of an overdose of barbiturates twenty years ago. *At around the same time the Face on Mars was first discovered!*

The Weekly World News article goes on to say that "scientists originally thought it was shifting sand or the play of light that was merely making it appear that the lips were moving."

That's a good first guess, don't you think?

"But upon further analysis, they concluded the movement was genuine." So they assembled a team of photoanalysts and lip readers to find out what the Face is trying to say.

"Progress has been slow," reported the article. "All they've been able to come up with so far are the nonsense sounds 'orgh,' 'rigu,' and 'agghk.'"

Now, I don't think we can blame a team of Soviet photoanalysts for not recognizing an American minor pop icon like Edie Sedgwick. Plus, they may have had other things on their minds at the time, like the fall of communism.

But if you so much as glance at these pictures, you will see that this face is not saying "orgh," "rigu," and "agghk."

And that it *is* saying "gu-aa-ay."

Gay.

So why are the photoanalysts lying? What kinds of fools do they take us for? They simply don't want this information delivered to the public!

Furthermore, the Orbitter took more than 2000 pictures of this strange phenomenon. What do the other photos, the ones they are *not* showing, say?

Probably something like, "I'm gay and proud!" Or "Lesbians of the world unite!"

But perhaps the most important question is: Why is Edie Sedgwick, of all people—who in life was pretty heterosexually self-destructive—announcing she's gay from the planet Mars? (Aside from the fact that Edie was sort of from Mars even when she was on Earth.)

I think Edie—with the aid of some lesbian interplanetary activist group—is sending a message to let Earth women know that they don't have to be a miserable het like she was. They can be happy and gu-aa-ay.

Think of it: We are witnessing an event of staggering historical importance. *This is the first posthumous coming out story from outer space.*

And that's not all. Edie Sedgwick was supposedly tragically in love with Bob Dylan, who purportedly treated her like dirt. She's the woman he addressed in his contemptuous song, *Like a Rolling Stone.* Remember? "How does it feel to be on your own/ with no direction home/ a complete unknown/ like a rolling stone...."

Well, obviously these mischievous outer space lesbians have a great sense of humor. They've made Edie a rolling stone, literally, and how she feels, now that she's on her own, like a rolling stone, is powerful and *gu-aa-ay.*

She's so happy she's a dyke, she's in orbit.

And American and Russian scientists have fabricated this elaborate coverup of the truth because they are scared shit-less of outer space lesbians!

So keep those giant lips a-movin', Edie! We read you loud and clear.

Okay, granted, it's still a theory. You may not be convinced until Lesbomania sniffs out further evidence. Which I'm confident we will.

But in the meantime—honestly, does that Face look like Elvis to you?

Back to Nature

I have been known to do Marlene Dietrich imitations with a kitchen towel draped over my head. So to avoid any misunderstanding, I should explain that when I say "I hate camping" I mean the outdoor kind—where people drive to some scenic area off the highway, smash metal stakes into the ground, crawl in and out of a flimsy nylon balloon, sleep on a hard, bumpy incline swatting mosquitos all night, cook prepackaged freeze-dried plasticized food, and tell themselves they are communing with nature. That kind of communing with nature is, for me, a guaranteed backache.

But long long ago, in a galaxy far away, I was a Girl Scout, and I actually looked forward to camping.

It was in Girl Scout Camp, in fact—the adolescent girl's introduction to "women-only space"—that I fell in love for the first time.

I was 15 and Bunky was 18. She was one of my counselors. I was a cigarette-puffing working class street kid to whom a tree was a foreign object, and she was a bright-faced farm-fed baby butch from the western hinterlands.

Obviously it was doomed from the start.

Oh, but how we'd stay up for hours by the romantic campfire light, long after the other campers had gone to bed. Bunky was a Mormon, of all things; she liked to talk about polygamy and angels and the Afterlife and visions of Brigham Young. I was a teenaged atheist, and I talked about evolution, the incomprehensibility of the vast mysteries of the universe, and the utter fallacy of all organized religion.

We argued our divergent cosmological views in passionate intellectual discourse—as only two young, horny lesbians who

80

don't know they are lesbians yet can do.

Then a tragic separation: I was advanced to another unit, and Bunky was no longer my counselor.

But (sigh) she'd show up at my new tent site late each night—secretly hiking through the woods without her flashlight so she wouldn't be seen—aquiver with some new theological argument she felt we urgently needed to discuss.

And every night (sigh) I got a goodnight kiss before Bunky dissolved back into the dark woods.

Now, we aren't talking Stonewall here, but *Stone Age*—it was 1962. I, who thought I was so smart, had no idea such promising possibilities as sexual/romantic relations between women existed among the vast mysteries of the universe I was always spouting on about.

And picture Bunky: this adorable butch number, wondering at eighteen when she was going to start getting interested in boys so she could join some patriarch's harem in Utah.

And the two of us, giving each other wide-eyed, longing looks.

Well, of course we were noticed. Some administrator called Bunky to the Headquarters Cabin and forbade her to talk to me anymore.

We both felt outraged. It was so unfair! All we'd been doing was trying to sort out the true nature of the universe! Sheesh! What did they *think* we were doing?

A light began to dawn.

What!?!

You mean...?!

Is it possible...??

Some people have such dirty minds!

Defiant, our secret meetings became all the more romantically charged.

At the end of the summer, Bunky pressed her yellow Girl Scout tie into my hand. I kept it as a treasure. I went back to the big city, and she was going off to South America to work for the Peace Corps.

But she came to visit me that September, just before she

left—for Bolivia or Uruguay, I really don't remember. She took me out to the World's Fair in Flushing, where we sheepishly held hands as she showed me around the Mormon pavilion.

When I got home, probably moony-eyed, my mother said with alarm, "*That's* the counselor you're always talking about?! She doesn't even look like a girl!"

You got it, Ma.

But I was scared to death by the enormous gulf between the messages society was giving me and the messages I was getting from my raging libido whenever I thought about Bunky.

I took on the project of becoming heterosexual—almost with a vengeance, you might say. Eventually, I even got married.

And I never saw Bunky again.

I keep hoping one day I'll run into her again at some women's music festival. She was, after all, an avid camper.

I've been out now for many years, but it was just five years ago—twenty-eight years after that innocent, sweet lesbo summer romance—that I finally said those explosive little words to my mother: "I'm a lesbian."

Believe it or not, my mother was shocked speechless. She really was.

But I could see the wheels spinning around in her head, and after what seemed like forever, she narrowed one eye, and said with conviction: "That camp counselor."

The persistence of memory!

But if my mother was looking for a place to put blame, I know that what I got from Bunky was, rather, a gift. Bunky gave me my first inkling of the real nature, not of the universe that we argued about so passionately, but of myself.

I hope that today, wherever she is, she remembers me in that way too.

What Becomes a Legend Most?

Liberace was the world's first "global village" homosexual. I mean, everybody in the *world* knew he was gay. Even people who didn't know what gay was.

If I could go back to the late 1950s in a time capsule, and ask someone in my parents' working class neighborhood in New York if they knew any homosexuals, I'm certain that after they got over their shock and had vigorously denied they knew *anyone* who was "that way," a light would dawn, and they'd smile and say—"Liberace!"

Even my mother knew he was gay. So did his, I bet.

And everybody *liked* him. People who would never be caught dead at a piano concert could see Liberace and feel they were getting some culture at the same time they were gaping at the glitz—which, in the '50s, was not nearly as glitzy as it got.

So, while in Las Vegas recently, a combination of curiosity and nostalgia compelled my lover and me to make a pilgrimage to the Liberace Museum.

Apparently a lot of people are curious and nostalgic. The museum—consisting of three small buildings, separated by a hot asphalt parking lot on a dismal desert road—is, we were told, the third largest tourist attraction in the state of Nevada.

And it was all there: the rhinestone-covered piano, the cars with the gold flecks, mirror tiles, acid-etched glass. The rhinestone roadster. Chandeliers all over the place. The world's *largest* rhinestone. Costumes encrusted with bugle beads and drop pearls. The Blackglama furs, mink, white fox. The platinum buttons with diamond letters spelling out Liberace's name.

The only thing missing was his real life.

Under glass at the "library building" was a book called *The Wonderful Private World of Liberace*. In it, says a blurb, Liberace describes, *in his own words*, the things that make him absolutely unique.

These things that make him unique include "his vacations, his homes and possessions, and his passion for shopping, cooking, and entertaining."

Pay no attention to that man behind the curtain.

Yet everybody *knew*. Even in my blue collar neighborhood, a million miles from Hollywood. It had come to us, loud and clear, right through that little television screen.

Among Liberace's collection of pianos was also a priceless hand-painted Pleyel concert grand once played by Chopin, and a Bosendorfer which had been played by Liszt, Schumann, and Brahms. They were sad reminders that this kid from Milwaukee was once a protégé of Paderewski, and had played with the Chicago Symphony when he was twelve years old.

What happened to the child prodigy? Liberace seemed to be doing some kind of a mirror trick: at the center of his persona, the two most important things about the man were there and at the same time were obviously missing: his music and his sexuality.

He was known as Mr. Showmanship.

In the museum's roomful of Liberace's stage costumes, each had a little plaque next to it describing the occasion on which he had worn it. One said: "Liberace wore this suit the first time he flew"—yes, that's right, flew—"at the finale of his 1976 'Salute to the Bicentennial'." This costume had a built-in harness so he could be hoisted 35 feet into the air.

His piano, however, remained earthbound.

There was one costume—a dark lavender suit with swirling pink and silver bugle beads—that had no plaque next to it. I imagined what it should have said: "This is the suit Liberace wore in gay and lesbian pride parades in New York, San Francisco, and Los Angeles." And I couldn't help thinking, as I stood looking at his glittering cars, how fantastic that rhinestone-covered roadster would have looked in a pride parade, with Liberace in his Blackglama waving to the thrilled onlookers.

It is a genuine pity he was never there with us. Mr. Showmanship—the highest-paid musician of all time—missed his greatest opportunity to fly above the crowd.

New Under the Sun

Back in the summer of 1969, I think I did see *something* on the TV news about riots occurring outside a local bar in Greenwich Village for several nights following Judy Garland's funeral. It didn't make much of an impression at the time. There were lots of riots in the Sixties. Especially in New York.

Much more clear in my memory is another news item I saw that summer. I was visiting my parents on Long Island. My father and I were glued to the TV set, watching the astounding spectacle of the first men walking on the moon.

For a long time before that, my father had been fond of repeating the old cliche, "There's nothing new under the sun." I think he said it often just to irk me; he was bitter and cynical, while I was in the Love Generation.

I saw my chance to gloat: "Nothing new under the sun, eh, Dad? What about this? Nothing like *this* has *ever* happened before."

My father was so absorbed by the flickering, high contrast images of astronauts bounding around in their space suits that he could barely speak.

Finally he turned to me and said simply, without a trace of his usual cynicism, "I never thought I'd live to see this day."

A few summers later, when the idea of gay pride parades was just taking hold, a gay male friend of mine told me he had decided to attend the Pride Parade in New York.

Just as a spectator. Just to be supportive. Just to see what it would be like.

This friend of mine was the first person who had ever come out to me. He was a high school music and drama teacher.

When I met him, Don was 52 and I was 16. He was the first adult I'd ever met who treated me like a person, an equal, instead of like a child. When I went on to college, we stayed in touch and eventually became close friends.

Several years before Stonewall he'd "confessed" to me that he was "queer as a three dollar bill."

It was from Don that I first learned about gay male culture as it existed then—the bars, the bathhouses, the slang, the secret signs of recognition—though in those days I never heard anyone use the word "gay" in a positive sense.

My friend Don had lived through nightmare years of repression, through psychoanalysts who told him he was sick and tried to "cure" him. His teaching career was almost ruined when he was entrapped and arrested by cops in a public men's room in the 1950s. His only daughter had disowned him when he'd told her he was a homosexual.

Though he'd become openly gay to all his friends, Don was still not able to see his sexuality as a source of pride.

The evening after this Gay Pride Parade in New York, I met him for coffee. Naturally the first thing I asked him was, "So how was the parade?"

Tears welled up in his eyes. He shook his head in awe.

"I never thought I'd live to see this day," he said.

He told me about his amazement at the sheer number of young people who'd been willing to be open and visible and claim their gay and lesbian identity. Who were not afraid or ashamed. He was so happy, he'd cried.

Accepting his own gayness as a positive part of himself, inspired by seeing so many others who were proud, was as unexpected for him as my father's notion that he might ever actually live to see men land on the moon.

Something new under the sun.

Looking over my own life's changes, and remembering what the world was like when I was a teenager, I can see that there's already much I never would have thought possible either, as a woman and as a lesbian.

I've marched in lesbian and gay pride marches myself now

for over a decade. In these grim days of plague, of continuing hatred against women and minorities, of escalating violence against gay men and lesbians, it can be difficult to think in terms of one person's life spanning a historical era, or what a sweeping view of history might inspire in those who live to witness it.

But I know that the ongoing revolution sparked by that little riot in Greenwich Village is one of the most significant things that has happened in my own life and in the lives of many of my friends.

Still, after marching in pride parades year after year, these celebrations can start to blur into one another. That first parade feeling of total exhilaration, of being so moved emotionally, can dwindle to become just another "gay holiday."

When I begin to feel that way, I call to mind all the lesbians and gay men around the world today for whom marching proudly and openly through their cities, cheered and applauded by well-wishers, is still as impossible as parading on the surface of the moon.

We march for them as well as for ourselves.

As we thump and roll and dance and sing and float our way through the streets, we are really moonwalking.

Because to be lesbians and gay men who are able to be out of the closet and proud is still something very, very new under the sun.

Alone at Last

Eighty-six years ago today—Sept. 18, 1905—an American icon was born in Stockholm. Like Marilyn and Elvis, Greta Gustafsson eventually became so famous that she needed only one name to evoke a mythology: Garbo.

Greta Garbo was beautiful, she was brilliant, she was extolled as the epitome of the desirable woman. When she quit Hollywood in 1941, she became a "puzzle," an "enigma," a "mystery." A "woman of secrets." She lived forty years "in hiding."

In all likelihood, she was a lesbian.

Part of her "mystery" resided in the fact that she was a beautiful woman who shunned the adoration of millions of admirers. Movie actresses just don't do that sort of thing.

After her death, *People Magazine* devoted a seven-page cover story to the "enigma" of Garbo. On the last page—after six pages about all the men in her life—the possibility of her lesbianism was directly addressed in one short three-sentence paragraph.

It read: "Rumors long swirled about Garbo's sexual preference, and with good reason. Silent film star Louise Brooks claimed to

Garbo (right) kisses Elizabeth Young in *Queen Christina* (1933)

have been intimate with her, as did the cosmopolitan aesthete Mercedes de Acosta. Curiously, throughout her life, Garbo referred to herself in masculine terms as a 'strapping young boy' or a 'bachelor.' "

That's it. In the proverbial nutshell. Note that even in a paragraph that clearly suggests she was a lesbian, the word "lesbian" is never once used.

Note that the word "lover" is never used either. Note also how the wording throughout the paragraph trivializes the topic.

Yet after focusing for six pages on the men in her life, the *People* article also comments: "Garbo seemed at times to regard men as excess baggage, preferring to go it alone."

Alone? Not exactly. She left her entire estate to her "housekeeper/companion" of thirty-five years.

Yes, it's *possible* Greta Garbo was not a closeted lesbian, but a recluse who chose never to marry, never to have children. Yet since the media always feels the need to heterize everybody, I think we are justified in our lesbozation of an "androgynous" cult icon like Garbo.

And her unprecedented, courageous, spectacular lesbian kiss in the 1933 movie *Queen Christina* assures Garbo's place in Lesbian Herstory, no matter what else is or is not ever revealed about her personal life.

There's that old feminist story of the man who goes up to two women in a restaurant and asks, "Are you ladies alone?" (25 years ago this was a common question asked of women who had no men with them, often as a prelude to joining them.) And the feminist response to the question: "No. We are not alone. We are with *each other.*"

I like to imagine Garbo, sitting at a dark table with another woman in some celestial Grand Hotel. Neither speaks. A debonair gentleman approaches and asks, "Are you ladies alone?" And through the smokey, cinematic haze, Garbo tosses that magnificent head, to wave him away, and takes the other woman's hand. In her deep, sexy voice, she says, "Yes, ve are alone. And ve vant to keep it that vey."

I'm Okay, You're Okay

12:30 in the afternoon, Pride Parade Sunday. My friend Paula and I were having a marvellous breakfast of omelettes and hashbrowns at an outdoor table at the Melrose Diner on Broadway, which is right along the parade route. The parade, as usual, was set to begin at 2 p.m.

The Melrose was crowded with gay men and lesbians. There was a spirit of anticipation. That brief pre-parade magic was in the air—everybody in the place seemed both gay and happy-gay to me. Perfect parade weather too, and from our table we could see that some people were already staking out curbside spots, an hour-and-a-half before the scheduled kickoff time.

Paula—who I sometimes refer to teasingly as "my corporate femme friend"—and I reminisced about pride parades of yesteryear. We updated each other on our love lives. We analyzed the continuing coming out process and other lesbyish topics.

During coffee, Paula excused herself to go to the ladies' room. When she returned, she had a strange, bemused look on her face.

"The most peculiar thing just happened while I was waiting on line for the bathroom," she said.

"What?"

"I almost got picked up—I think."

There were three or four women in front of her when she joined the line, Paula told me. "I was minding my own business—well, actually, I was standing behind this really cute butchy dyke, admiring her great muscle tone," she said, "when this very old, very straight little woman came out of the bathroom." She stopped right in front of Paula, stood there, looked up at her, and peered into her face.

"You uh-kay?" the woman asked her in a thick accent that Paula couldn't identify.

"Why, yes, I'm fine, thank you," said my ever-polite friend Paula—though she wondered why this stranger was so concerned about her well being.

"You uh-kay?" the woman asked again.

"I'm fine," said Paula. "Really."

But the woman persisted, asking again. "She was very small and frail and her face was very wrinkled. She had to be 85 or 90," said Paula. After answering several more times, and feeling more and more self-conscious, Paula suddenly realized that the woman might not be saying "You okay?" but rather "*You a gay?*"

"Oh! Am I *gay?*" asked Paula.

The old woman nodded her head, still peering at her quizzically.

"My first reaction," Paula told me, "was to get defensive and say, 'Why do you ask?' But then I thought, Hey, this is Pride Day. She's probably not used to seeing so many gay men and lesbians around."

So Paula simply answered the woman, "Yes, I am gay," and smiled.

The old woman smiled back at Paula. "Me too," she confided happily, then covered her mouth with her hand and tittered as if they now shared an amusing little secret.

"Gosh," I said, glancing around the restaurant, "I want to see this woman. Where did she go? What was she wearing?"

Paula had to think for a minute. "She looked totally straight. I mean, she couldn't have looked straighter. Polyester pedal pushers and a floral print top, I think. To tell you the truth, Jorjet," she said, "I noticed the butchy dyke in a lot more detail. She was tall, tan, with brown eyes and was wearing a sleeveless top, tight jeans, and these killer tennis shoes. She had this cute smile, and full lips." Paula sighed. "And that muscle tone..."

"The little old woman looked at me and said, 'You are-a very-a beau-tee-fool,' and winked at me."

"No! She came on to you?!"

"Well, I don't know," said Paula. "Just then this younger woman, who might have been her daughter, came over and took the old woman by the arm, and said to her, like she was a child, 'Come on, we gotta go now...' and led the little old lady away."

Leaving Paula to wonder what on earth that had all been about.

"We really are everywhere, aren't we?" she said.

Paula and I met several of our friends across the street just as the parade was beginning, and told them about the mystery lady in the polyester pedal pushers. We asked them all, "You uh-kgay?"

Indeed they were.

On Gay Pride Sunday, I'm okay, you're okay, I'm a gay, you're a gay, and—for that brief magical time when we gather and openly celebrate our lives—everybody's gay, anybody can be gay, and everything's really okay.

Dykes Along The Nile

The only woman in the history of Ancient Egypt who ever ascended to the throne as Pharaoh was Hatshepsut. Historians have called her the "Queen Elizabeth of Egypt" because her 16-year reign (beginning in 1472 BC) was characterized by peace, prosperity, and high culture—a Golden Age, generations before King Tut.

This is historical fact. You can look her up in the encyclopedia for yourself.

Hatshepsut changed the ending of her name from the female to the male ("- ut") form and wore male clothing. People referred to her as "he."

Historians say that by assuming a male image she kept her power in an otherwise totally male power structure.

So far no historian has suggested that maybe she *liked* wearing men's clothes.

Though her father was himself a Pharaoh, Hatshepsut claimed to have been conceived when her mother, Queen Ahmose, was visited one night by the principal god, Amon-Re. It was typical for ancient rulers to claim divine parenthood as a justification for their right to the throne, but there's a strikingly vivid erotic passage in the ancient literature describing, from Ahmose's point of view, how nice it felt to have sex with god.

Hatshepsut married her brother—as was the royal custom, since the divine spark of Maat, they believed, came only through the female side, and they wanted to keep it in the royal family. He died, but not before fathering, by another wife, a son who grew up to give Hatshepsut grief and become her successor: the warrior Thutmose III (known as "The

Napoleon of Egypt"), who reigned for half a century and conquered foreign lands by force. Thutmose III tried to erase Hatshepsut's name from history by chipping it out of the monuments she erected, smashing her statues and sphinxes, and defacing her elegant temple at Dier al Bahri.

Apart from these and a few other basic facts, most of the details of Hatshepsut's life are lost.

I think Hatshepsut should be credited not only as the only woman Pharaoh, but also as the world's first lesbian head-of-state.

As far as I'm concerned, Hatshepsut is the first big-time dyke in history. And we are talking ancient: Hatshepsut was bopping along the banks of the Nile in the 18th Dynasty's fashion equivalent of a tuxedo during the fifteenth century BC—900 years before Sappho ever chased a skirt on Lesbos.

Of course, Hatshepsut couldn't have called herself a "lesbian" since that particular word hadn't been invented yet. Lesbos wouldn't become famous for its women-loving-women for another thousand years.

An entire gallery in the Egyptian Wing at the Metropolitan Museum of Art in New York is devoted to Hatshepsut. On one side of the room she's dressed in women's clothes, on another side she's dressed as the Pharaoh in full male regalia including the royal false beard, symbol of kingship.

All in all, it's quite a sight to see.

Since so little is known about her life, and yet her reign stands out so uniquely in history, imaginative people have been eager and willing to fill in the gaps. Lesbomania has suffered through several badly written heterosexual historical romance novels in which the great Pharaoh Hatshepsut becomes silly putty in the arms of her chief architect, Senenmut. And even worse, we've suffered through some overtly sexist and tacitly homophobic scholarly accounts of her reign. So Lesbomania wants to balance the record and set things, uh, uh-straight.

Upon close examination of the extant literary texts and monumental art of Ancient Egypt, Lesbomania has been able to reinterpret Hatshepsut's Golden Age, and to formulate the theory that it was indeed a glorious Golden Age of Lesbian Culture.

The texts of the period employ metaphors that are obviously part of an elaborate lesbian code: they frequently use such words as "deltas" and "canals" that are, once you know how to read them, unquestionably references to lesbian lovemaking.

One actual ancient text says "The moist delta is overflowing, and I ride upon your flood."

Does that resonate with anything in your experience?

Another says, "Dip thy fingers into the pool," and goes on to say that if you do this, it will "cause the ripples to spread."

Even the nonlesbomaniacal mind should be able to get the allusion—spreading ripples is undoubtedly a thinly disguised reference to female orgasms. You might argue that it could still be interpreted as heterosexual—but note that it's not a rod or a pole or a wick or an oar that is to be dipped, but an invitation to "dip thy fingers."

And another passage reads: "Pleasant is the channel which your hand hath digged." The inference couldn't be clearer if this were a lesbian sex manual. Which perhaps it was: the Ancient Egyptian equivalent of the *Joy of Lesbian Sex* !

A wall relief at the Dier al Bahri temple depicts one of Hatshepsut's royal barges, while another ancient text says "I voyage downstream and sail through the canal. I desire to go where the tents are set up at the opening of the mouth of the Mertiu."

Now, the word "tents" is a clear giveaway for any lesboarcheologist. Putting image and texts together, we can surmise that Hatshepsut hosted some wild royal lezboat celebrations, something like Ancient Egyptian Olivia Cruises. Then the sailing party would land at the women's music festival at the mouth of the Mertiu, a place where everyone has pitched their tent in the sand for the lesbian gathering.

At the women's music festival itself, of course, very likely the women would have had women's music onstage, not very different from the way they do today. Hieroglyphs depicting women's music groups have been discovered; unimaginative scholars would have you believe these were slave-girl musicians, when in fact they were probably the ancient equivalent of a group like Betty, performing for the appreciative all-woman audiences who applauded them.

The festie-goers would also buy souvenirs and gifts for their friends. The scarabs and other small artifacts, found in profusion in museums around the world today, were probably created and sold by New Kingdom lesbian craftswomen in the crafts areas. Some sex toys and other paraphernalia would also be discreetly displayed and sold for women interested in that kind of thing. Since rubber was unknown, hippopotamus hide and other naturally elastic products were probably the materials of choice.

And of course these women would be interested in lesbian literature.

"She turned her smiling face toward the delta"—that word delta again—"and entered the thicket laden with fruit redder than the ruby."

Yes, that's what it says: "entered the thicket laden with fruit redder than the ruby."

This passage clearly demonstrates to any lesbian-minded individual the mind-boggling continuity in our lesbian literary tradition over the millenia: from the ruby fruit thicket to the ruby fruit jungle!

Another ancient inscription reads, "I see the sweet cake, and it tastes like salt." A contradiction in terms? Not for lesbians.

From the ancient texts, it also appears there was a debate going on between ancient earthdykes and long-ago lipstick lesbians at the festival about whether or not to use cosmetics: "Shall you put powders on thy lovely face, and paint your eyes with kohl?" says one indignant voice, which goes on to an accusation of using scented products: "Must thee anoint thyself with unguents?"

Another ancient fragment reads "...spending thy nights at the crocodile pit with the maiden who keeps watch over the vineyards..." The Crocodile Pit may very well have been the name of an ancient lesbian bar, perhaps in Hatshepsut's capital city at Thebes. The maiden keeping watch over the vineyards could be a poetic allusion to the bartender.

"I see my sister coming and my heart rejoices." No need for explanations here.

"Her breasts are like love-apples. My arms are opened wide to embrace her, and my heart rejoices. If I kiss her and her lips are open" (getting rather graphic here) "I am happy even without drinking beer."

Obviously, there were 12-step meetings at the festival.

Another hieroglyph has mistakenly been identified as Hatshepsut next to her Cartouche—but any lesbian familiar with women's culture today will instantly recognize that it is an elegant, tasteful representation of Ancient Egyptian lesbians waiting patiently in line for the portajane 𓇋𓄿𓎼𓃀𓂋𓈖 at the Mertiu women's music festival.

Alas, the Lesbian Golden Age of Egypt died along with Hatshepsut. The monumental statues in the Metropolitan Museum and in other museums around the world were reconstructed piece by piece from smashed fragments found at Hatshepsut's temple. Thutmose had them all broken.

While there may not be much satisfaction in falling in love with someone who's been dead for 36 hundred years, Hatshepsut is a major heartthrob. And I hope to finish my own herstorical romance novel, complete with graphic lesbian sex scenes aboard the royal barge, before somebody else beats me to it. As you can see, some of the dialogue can be taken verbatim from the actual ancient hieroglyphs.

Obviously there's a pulp-novel market in Lesbo-Egyptology out there just waiting to be tapped.

And even those backward-looking archaeologists (but then I suppose they all would have to be) who would hesitate to conclude that this powerful woman Pharaoh was a lesbian based on Lesbomania's evidence, even *they* will be unable to deny that, at the very least, she's the world's first documented female-to-male cross-dresser.

And that she looks very, very dykey in that Pharaonic beard.

Through the Looking Glass

Let's suppose for just a moment that we lived in a world where "everyone" was gay or lesbian.

In other words, in this looking-glass world, about one person in ten, statistically, is actually straight. But nevertheless, many gays and lesbians argue that straight people can't possibly be a whole ten percent of the population. "Look around you," they say. "Just about 'everyone' is gay or lesbian."

Yet in this world, "everyone" knew that the straight minority was persecuted and, by a peculiar process of willful ignorance, was constantly made invisible. Suppose, since "everyone" was gay or lesbian, a HUNDRED PERCENT of what was presented on TV, on the radio, in popular music, in advertisements, everywhere, was geared to the ninety percent of the population who was "everybody."

Suppose that straights were often ostracized just for being honest about their sexuality.

For example, if a teenage boy, after many sleepless nights, decided to tell his folks the truth:

"Ma, I like to sleep with girls."

And the family (two lesbian mothers and two gay male uncles—one of whom was the boy's biological father) reacted with wailing and gnashing of teeth.

If Mom, stricken, cried, "Oh, son! How could you?!" and turned to her lover, sobbing, "Honey, where did we go wrong?"

Suppose that when the existence of straight people was admitted, albeit reluctantly, it was usually to revile and ridicule them.

For example, if a fourteen year-old girl was caught secretly reading a heterosexual romance novel, and all her peers, well-adjusted gay boys and dykelets, jeered at her and called her names (though later, one of the boys who taunted her confided that he, too, was straight—and maybe they could get together...?).

Suppose that wherever they went, straight people were pressured to conform to the gay "norm" or hide.

For example, if when a man and woman walked through the park holding hands, others whispered and gave them dirty looks, and gay couples making out on the grass accused them of "flaunting" their sexuality. But even when the couple went quietly to their own few straight bars, they risked being assaulted by "straight-bashers."

Suppose that 750,000 straight people gathered in the U.S.A.'s capital to prove to the gay world that straight people did exist.

Suppose it was the largest civil rights protest in the country's history, but the event was buried by the gay media.

And that the powerful American media totally ignored the plight of all the straight people in countries where just to be straight was to risk imprisonment or death.

Okay. Now, WHAT IF, despite all the stigma, denial, ostracism, and persecution, people declared that they were who they were anyway, did what they did anyway—and many were *even proud*?

Imagine "everyone's" incredulity! "Everyone" might ask themselves:

When we've campaigned so hard to prove this minority doesn't exist, and told them that when they do exist, they shouldn't—*how can there be this many of them?*

But that question couldn't be asked in this world. It would expose the fear underlying the source of the repression.

And it would lead to another question: If, with nothing but negative messages and zero recognition, ten percent are this way now—good grief! How many might there be if there were no stigma attached? What would happen?

"Everyone's" assumptions about what the world was like would have to change. Even the definition of who was "everyone" would have to change.

Unthinkable!

Ergo, "everyone" should do like "we" do, and want what "we" want, and that's all there is to it!

Now, let's suppose for just a moment that we lived in a world in which "everyone" was a woman—except for the five people out of ten who were male...

Ex to the Nth

Eight lesbians, including me, are sitting at a long table at The Bagel, a restaurant on Broadway. It's one of those impromptu kinds of get-togethers after an event we've all attended. Most of us have known each other for a long time.

Directly across the table from me is an ex lover of mine—the only ex lover of mine in the present group. She smiles—tentatively. I smile back—tentatively. She and I are just in the beginning stages of being able to be friends again.

To my ex's left is her current lover, someone I have known for years, though not closely.

My ex has also, it occurs to me, had a passing fling with the woman who is at the far end of my side of the table.

Come to think of it, my ex's new lover, years ago, had a long, intense relationship with the same woman that my ex had the more recent fling with.

Hmmmm. As I munch my toasted bagel contemplatively, I begin mentally calculating the romantic and sexual connections of the women here.

That is, the ones I know about.

My ex's current lover has slept with at least two other women at the table. It's not like this is any secret. She had a brief but reportedly very hot relationship with the woman sitting diagonally across from me to my left.

The woman sitting diagonally across from me to my left had been the longtime lover of the woman at the end of the table at the time of the hot affair, and the woman at the end of the table had been extremely upset about it.

But that's all water under the bridge.

More recently—this is to say several years ago—the woman at the end of the table had been lovers with the woman directly on my left.

The woman directly on my left and the woman at the end of the table had a particularly nasty breakup. That was before the woman on my left began seeing her current lover, who was the roommate of the woman at the end of the table.

The current lover of the woman directly on my left was also once lovers with the woman sitting diagonally across from me to the left *and* with the woman sitting diagonally across from me to the right, that is, my ex's current lover.

Sitting on the far end of the other side of the table is the current lover of the one who had the long-term relationship with the woman on my end of the table, and the hot fling with my ex's latest.

As far as I know, the woman on the far-end far-side has not slept, ever, with anyone else at the table except the woman sitting next to her.

I vividly remember when these two got together because my lover at the time was her current lover's roommate. The screaming and moaning that came from that bedroom went on at all hours. They are now solidly a Couple—they've already celebrated their second anniversary.

Directly on my right is a woman I know only slightly; we have been to a few of the same parties. Her claim to fame is that she came out on the Oprah show. The lone exception, she is the only person at the table who, as far as I know, has had no sexual connections with anyone else at the table.

As far as I know.

But as she begins describing her breakup with her most recent ex, I realize that her most recent ex is also a big-time ex of one of my exes.

Now we are getting to second-order relationships, and my head is beginning to spin.

What tangled webs we weave.

And they think—whoever "they" are—that lesbians don't

have as much sex as straight people. Where are the sociologists and sexologists when a group like this is around, so ripe for a statistical analysis?

Everybody is chatting and eating and giving each other a taste of their dishes. Soups, cake, salad.

But I am quiet, brooding as I sip my coffee. As a matter of fact, I am appalled. This lesbian community is so ingrown! Isn't there anybody who hasn't slept with somebody who has slept with somebody else I know?

Then I think to myself: Wait a minute. This is really quite remarkable: How many heterosexuals could be involved in this many intertwined relationships on so many levels over time and still be able to sit at the same table with each other, much less enjoy each other's company?

If this were a table full of hets with this much sexual history, they probably would have killed each other by now. They certainly wouldn't be passing around rice pudding with cinnamon so everyone could have a taste.

Maybe it's true that lesbians tend to have ugly break-ups—but after the arguing and the bad scenes and the not-being-on-speaking-terms interval, there is still some kind of a bond, a loyalty—even if it's only a fond acknowledgment of a shared history—that often prevails after the pain subsides.

Not always, admittedly. But often.

This meal is, I think, living proof of it.

Six months later:

A late-night post-show gathering at Leona's, an Italian restaurant in Rogers Park. There are ten lesbians this time, including five of us who were at the Bagel dinner.

The Couple have celebrated their third anniversary by now. My ex and her new lover have broken up, but they are both here, trying to be friends.

The woman diagonally across from me remarks that an ex of hers and an ex of mine have just begun seeing each other. "I guess that makes us family," she says.

The woman who sat directly on my left at the Bagel is not here. She and her lover split up and are not on speaking

104

terms. But her ex is here—she's sitting on my right. She is my new lover.

Directly across from me is my new lover's old ex, who is visiting from out of town. She was my new lover's lover before my lover was lovers with her most recent lover before me.

If you follow.

My lover and her old ex have recently gotten back on speaking terms. Which is nice for everybody, since most of us have known both of them for years.

My lover has also, it occurs to me, been lovers with at least two other women at the table...

I begin calculating our romantic and sexual connections.

This time it is so complicated that I have to make a flow-chart on scrap paper, with circles and arrows and dotted lines.

We chat and laugh and pass around food.

Is it like this everywhere, or is this a Chicago sort of thing?

In any case, our relationships appear to be ex-panding.

Ex-ponentially.

Practice Makes Perfect

The "gays in the military" issue has become a large-scale public debate, constantly in the news right now. As a result, some politicians and newscasters have been forced to say out loud, over and over, in a polite manner, certain words that they previously might only have whispered (or shouted).

So, as a public service to anyone who has had trouble saying queer words in an even, matter-of-fact way, without fear, hostility, or accusation, Lesbomania offers you the following helpful hints and practical exercises.

GAY. A simple one-syllable word that rhymes with "day," though a few newscasters seem to hesitate or gag on the opening "G."

Practice repeating a strong "guh" sound, from deep in the throat. When this has been thoroughly mastered, then move on to the "ay." "Ay" has traditionally been an easy sound for sports fans and good students. For a more advanced exercise, try repeating the entire word in front of the mirror.

MAN. Say "M" as in "Mmmmm, good," and "aan" as in "tan." Even though men, one would think, are perfectly capable of stringing together these two one-syllable words into the phrase "gay man," a gender difference is noticeable here: none of the women in the Senate seem to have any trouble at all with the phrase, while some of their many male counterparts have been having a very hard time with it.

LESBIAN. This word, for some reason (more syllables?), is much tougher for many people to say than "gay." Kate Clinton has noted that some women find it impossible to say the word "lesbian" even when their mouths are full of one.

The English letter "L" is taken from the Greek letter "lambda," which the Ancient Greeks themselves had no difficulty whatsoever in pronouncing. Linguistically, "L" is classified as a "liquid" sound, meaning that there is some obstruction of the airstream in the mouth, but not enough to cause friction. In other words, it's a wet and smooth consonant.

To produce this liquidy sound, stretch and elevate the tongue slightly until the tip touches the back of the top front teeth, or, if one is more adventurous, stretch even further and touch the soft, smooth, moist skin of the middle of the upper lip. Hold the tongue in this position and utter an expressive moan from low in the throat: "Lllllll...."

Practice, practice.

Try repeating the sentence: "Lesbians lick light leaping lolling luscious lurching labia, tra-la-la-la-la!" This permits repetition of the "L" sound in combination with each of the vowel sounds a-e-i-o-u and y. The more quickly you can say it, the more you will get practice in the gentle flicking of the tongue, useful in building overall flexibility and muscle control of the organ.

Heterosexual women will also appreciate men who do this exercise conscientiously.

Next we combine the "L" sound with the sound "ezz." No, it's not pronounced "less," though the somewhat silly, confusing spelling, "lessie bars," in the old pulp novels of Ann Bannon would certainly suggest otherwise.

Admittedly the "z" sound is not an easy one, but can be very intellectually stimulating to produce. Try going "zzzz" until your head vibrates. Pretend you are a bee. Then say "Bee" and you have, voila, the next sound mastered as well.

While "an" is easy for almost everyone, "bee-yan" is problematic. Remember that it is pronounced as two syllables, not one (as it is, for example, in "soybean"). Practice by saying aloud, clearly, over and over, "Lez-bee-YAN, Lez-bee-YUN, Lez-bee-YIN." One can do this at odd moments, while waiting for the cameras to roll in the studio, for instance, or waiting for a conference with the President.

HOMOSEXUAL. Yes, this is a long word, but nevertheless it seems to be preferred by many media people and politicians to the shorter, so much more easily pronounceable "gay." Some have protested that the phrase "gay and lesbian" is too cumbersome, but on closer examination it is exactly the same number of syllables—five—as "ho-mo-sex-u-al."

"Ho" is very simple. It begins with a voiceless glottal fricative and it rhymes with blow, a bilabial plosive.

"Mo" is equally simple—as in Mo, Larry and Curly, Mo of *Dykes to Watch Out For*, and *Mo' Better Blues*. But "sex" and "sex-u-al" are, in general, still psychologically difficult words for many Americans to utter, thanks to our Puritan heritage. The "X" in "sex" is a composite "K" sound and "S" sound: you can spell it s-e-c-k-s. Perhaps you have heard the radio commercials that claim you can learn Spanish in 30 days by remembering that "s-o-c-k-s" spells "Eso si que es" ("That's what it is")? Well, with a simple variant mnemonic, the word "sexual" presents the slightly more philosophical question: Es y si que es 'shoe' al?" (It is and yes what is 'shoe' to the?"). Shoes and socks—an easy way to remember!

Some congressmen, particularly those from the South, can learn to say "sex" in a conversational manner by picking out and combining sounds of words already familiar to them, like "segregation" and "extremist."

And notice that the last syllable in homosexual, "ual," is pronounced similarly to "You-all"—also quite familiar to Southerners already.

QUEER. Some news announcers who had no problem saying "Ku-wait" during the Gulf War have been having infinitely more difficulty on the word "Ku-weer."

You can learn to say it ku-wickly and evenly if you just remember that, like Kuwait, Queer is a Nation with valuable resources that has been under threat from hostile powers—and it's a small, peaceful nation that many people believe is well worth fighting for.

See? Not so difficult after all!

To name something is to acknowledge that it exists. So Lesbomania wants to encourage all you politicians, media people, religious leaders, armed forces personnel, community leaders: Keep Practicing!

As a final exercise: Now that you've become more comfortable with the words "Gay Man," "Lesbian," "Homosexual," and "Queer," repeat them all again, until you can say them completely conversationally—with not a trace of fear or malice in your heart.

108

Shangri-La-La

Nestled high in the mountains of northern California, shrouded in fog, is the hidden cave of the great lesbian guru, Mamarama.

Here, Mamarama sits in lotus position on a bed of healing crystals, contemplating the eternal, and practicing the ancient art of yoga to release the powerful lesbian energy that smolders in her color-coded chakras.

Recently, Lesbomania made the hazardous trek up the snow-topped mountains to meet the living legend and watch her in action.

Mamarama, we discovered, lives humbly in a humid, temperature-controlled cave, its walls decorated with lesbian-made macramé.

Her simple entertainments consist of listening to old Meg Christian and Kay Gardner albums, which she plays over and over. Each Sunday she holds a potluck for her followers.

New Age lesbians and other seekers of wisdom who have heard of Mamarama come from around the world to ask her guidance and to find answers to their vexing questions about life and lesbians.

Sometimes a prudent silence is the only answer they receive.

"O Great Mamarama," asked a nervous woman with blond stringy hair, the first in line for the day, "What is a lesbian?"

Mamarama looked at the woman in silence for a full five minutes.

Then suddenly the woman leaped up, shouting, "Oh! I see what you mean!"

Grateful for having been thus enlightened, she left a small herbal offering in the vestibule of the cave, and went on her way smiling.

Sometimes, in the pedagogic manner of other guru masters, Mamarama answers a question with another question.

A group of leather dykes and radical separatists, locked in seemingly unresolvable philosophical opposition, came to Mamarama to settle their dispute.

They all bowed respectfully (the S/M dykes kneeling) and asked, "O Great Mamarama, what is S/M?"

Mamarama shifted her weight on the bed of healing crystals and frowned. "What isn't?" she said mysteriously.

Both the S/M dykes and the separatists went away satisfied with her answer.

A gay man came to ask about monogamy and nonmonogamy.

"You must look deep within yourself for the answer, my son," said Mamarama, in a kind voice, shaking her head. "Or, you could journey over the next mountain, and ask at the summer palace of the great gay male guru Ramalama. You can call for his door-to-door limo service in the vestibule of my cave."

A woman wearing a necktie and a wraparound skirt, with a deeply puzzled look on her face, was next.

"O Great Mamarama," she began, "Is the butch/femme phenomenon that is enjoying a resurgence in some parts of the lesbian community today a throwback to mimicking heterosexual sex roles of the 1950s, or is it rather an expression of an integral element of the duality of the human sexual complex?"

"Yes," said Mamarama.

"Where do lesbians come from?" asked another pilgrim.

"Why, from outer space, of course," said Mamarama. "Don't you read 'Lesbomania'?"

Sometimes Mamarama tires of answering questions that are asked over and over again.

"O Great Mamarama," a team of academic researchers

asked, their arms stuffed with journal articles, "please tell us, what do lesbians do?"

"Lesbians do everything."

"We mean in bed."

"Oh, that again," she replied, sighing. "Don't get me started."

Mamarama lifted her hands, touched her fingertips together, smiled, and softly began humming: *"Filling up and spilling over, it's an endless waterfall...."*

The audience was over for the day. Her aura radiating deep purple, Mamarama resumed her solitary meditations.

Heart to Heart

Some forms of intellectual dishonesty are so sickening they're not even worthy of satire, so this will not be a funny column.

I was there when the AIDS Name Project Memorial Quilt was first unfurled at the 1987 March on Washington. During that year 4,100 people—overwhelmingly gay men—died of AIDS. That same year, 41,000 people—overwhelmingly women—died of breast cancer. Going by the standard one-in-ten estimate, one tenth of those women were lesbians. Thus, in 1987, *almost exactly* as many lesbians died of breast cancer as gay men died of AIDS.

I have been writing for the gay press since before anyone ever heard of AIDS, and, like most people in the gay and lesbian community, I have a long personal list of dead and dying friends. It disgusts me to have to resort to a comparison of "body counts" between diseases, because our grief and loss should never and can never be reduced to raw, faceless numbers. But the writer of a recent "Boys Town" column claimed there are no "lesbian-specific health problems that deserve the kind of mobilization we've seen around AIDS."

If as many lesbians are dying of breast cancer as gay men are dying of AIDS, why are lesbians not allowed to consider breast cancer among lesbians a community issue, an epidemic "deserving" of their time and energy?

"Boys Town" contends that unless a health malady takes "special aim" at lesbians, it's "irrelevant" to the gay community. This is just misogynistic, slippery logic with no substance.

The fact that heterosexual IV-drug users and others, as well as gay men, are dying of AIDS isn't used as an argument to belittle gay men and lesbians who are fighting AIDS. Just because straight women are also dying of breast cancer does not negate the fact that breast cancer is a growing, lethal, horrifying threat to lesbians. Because many women with breast cancer are in an older age group than those dying of AIDS doesn't make their death not death.

"Boys Town" says: "There are no health problems that threaten lesbians in a statistically significant way any more than they threaten all women."

Even if that were true, it would be a facetious way of ignoring lesbian health issues. But "Boys Town" is not only wrong-headed about this claim, it's just plain wrong.

According to Dr. Suzanne Haynes of the National Cancer Institute, currently lesbians are at an eighty percent higher risk for breast cancer than straight women, and lesbians have an eighty percent higher mortality rate from breast cancer.

We are not talking small numbers here. At the present time, one woman in eight will get breast cancer (up from one in nine just last year). As alarming as that projection is, the risk for lesbians is greater, and may even be as high as *one in three.*

AIDS is a disease that still has no cure—but it's now known how to protect yourself against contracting it. Breast cancer can frequently be "cured" (though amputation is not the same thing as a true cure) when caught in its early stages—but its cause is glaringly unknown. (Despite what you may have heard to the contrary, eighty percent of women with breast cancer today have no known family history of the disease, and seventy percent have no known risk factor.) Breast cancer is beginning to strike more and more women under thirty.

I don't want to in any way discount the intense homophobia that lies behind the bureaucratic inertia on AIDS research and care, and I want to underscore the vital importance of finding a swift cure for HIV infection. But I'm also putting sexist fuckheads on notice: Stop trying to divide us according to your hierarchy of prejudices. Stop belittling lesbians who are trying to help themselves and other lesbians.

Nobody has cornered the market on grief—or on survival either.

Let me repeat this: Lesbians are at an alarmingly high level of risk for breast cancer. Breast cancer is a lesbian issue. Arguing that it is not—because "women who are not lesbians also get breast cancer"—is what is really "irrelevant" to gay men and lesbians who care about each other's lives.

No Place Like Home

My nice old Sweet Home Chicago cheap-rent apartment building in the Lakeview neighborhood is being sold. This means I must join the small army of people combing the streets right now in search of "for rent" signs.

I'm packing up all my voluminous stuff—the accumulated contents of five years of living in a six-room apartment—including ten bookcases with roughly three thousand books and goddess knows how many magazines and periodicals. Not to mention all the assorted Lesbiana: ornamental teapots, bulbous vases, and other impractical, heavy, yet fragile ceramics that I've brought back from various women's music festivals like safari trophies.

Even more difficult than packing all this stuff up, though, is finding a place to move it to.

As a professional lesbian writer, I need an apartment big enough to house my personal lesbian and gay archives, my complete collections of lesbian periodicals, my darkroom equipment, my office complete with file cabinets stuffed with files from the hundreds of gay and lesbian newspaper articles I've written.

Then there's my hobby: all the crafts tools and paraphernalia I use to produce my handmade lesbian refrigerator magnets.

And it has to be a place where I can also keep Spyke, my darling, furry, floppy-eared, doe-eyed, cuddly little cat-size dog.

And since I'm a lesbian writer—not exactly a top salary career—it has to be an apartment that's cheap, to boot.

My girlfriend drove me around to check some places out. In an iffy neighborhood, we came across a promising "for rent" sign.

"A lot of lesbians live around here," she assured me. "Dykes who've been pushed out of Lakeview since the rents there have gone up."

The place was certainly run down, but I don't mind that. In fact, "Run Down" is the decor that matches all my furniture.

But I think there's a definite line between "Run Down" and "Fire Trap," and I wasn't sure which category this place fell into.

I was trying to decide. Eyeing the exposed electrical wiring that hung out of an unusable light socket. The scatter of dead cockroaches that dotted the kitchen countertops. The unsalvageable vermin-breeding rugs that the landlord assured me he was removing at great expense to himself.

"What're the floors like underneath?" I asked him.

"Who knows?" the landlord said philosophically, shrugging.

No, Toto, we're not in Lakeview anymore.

He pointed out two small stained glass windows in the living room as a favorable feature. I opened one. It was haphazardly boarded up on the other side with plywood.

"You would be wanting to rent...the two of you together?" he asked, peering at us.

"Just me," I said, "and my teeny-weeny, quiet, well-behaved, itsy bitsy pet....dog."

He frowned. "Are you two sisters?"

"No," we said in unison.

"Oh. Friends, then?" he asked with a touch of sarcasm in his voice.

"Girlfriends," I told him.

A few awkward moments of silence passed.

It hadn't even dawned on me, living for the last five years in a gay-positive atmosphere, that on top of all the upheaval, I'd have to worry about whether my new landlord would be a homophobic sleazebag.

I know that it's against the law to discriminate against gays and lesbians now in Chicago, but who wants to live somewhere where it's a problem? Where I'd have to show discretion in displaying my dykey artwork. Where I'd feel paranoid wearing lesbian T-shirts in front of the neighbors.

Shit. After five years, I don't know if I can adjust to the real, homophobic world.

I do know that I don't want to.

If only I could click my heels, and find someplace affordable that's big, in a reasonably safe neighborhood, that allows pets, maybe even one that has a gay or lesbian landlord.

There's no place like home.

So where the heck did I pack those ruby slippers?

Zoo Story

I read in the *Chicago Tribune* that the San Francisco Zoo conducted a Valentine's Day adults-only "sex tour" of the zoo animals for $15 a ticket. The tour guides talked about contraception and the "animals that use birth control" (an interesting way to put it) at the zoo, and answered "questions about monogamy, homosexuality and foreplay."

Among the tour highlights: "two lesbian, nearly monogamous penguins."

I was rather mystified by the phrase "nearly monogamous" in reference to lesbian penguins. Did it mean they mostly had sex with each other, but once in a while snuck a fuck with a male penguin? Or sometimes "slept with" other female penguins?

"Maybe," said my friend Marcy, "it means they are in a committed monogamous relationship, except when they attend lesbian penguin music festivals."

So I called the SF Zoo to clarify the sexual behavior of these lesbian penguins.

I was connected with a cheerful zoo spokesperson named Susie Campbell.

"I read about how on Valentine's Day you gave a special tour..." I began.

"Our sex tour!" she said enthusiastically. "Yes!"

This woman clearly enjoys her job.

"This is the second year we've done this tour," she said. "We got a great response last year, so we advertised it more this year, and the response was phenomenal." Most of the tour, she said, centered around the topic of animal birth control.

But it turns out the *Trib* had the penguin thing all wrong.

"The article said you have 'two lesbian nearly monogamous penguins,'" I said, but she stopped me right there.

"It's *geese*," she corrected, quite emphatically. "We have two lesbian *geese*."

Penguins, she told me, are "among the most romantic animals in the zoo," but alas, the "nearly-monogamous" pair they have are heterosexual.

Bummer.

"But in the tour," she continued, "we also talk about the two lesbian geese we have here in the zoo which have laid, oh, god, about fifty unfertilized eggs for each other."

"Sounds like they're in love," I said.

"Oh, yes! And they don't need to mate with a male in order to have eggs, you know. There's never been a male in contact with them," said Ms. Campbell. "Keepers have been watching them roost together every day for the past three years."

"So the lesbian geese are also 'nearly monogamous'?"

"They're *inseparable*," said Ms. Campbell.

Awwww, how sweet! I can see these lesbian geese being approached by some smug, swaggering gander. "Quack off," they tell him, in no uncertain terms.

The SF Zoo, she said, has no gay male animals that she knows of (which I thought was strange, but I guess she'd know—it would probably be difficult for an animal to be in the closet in a zoo). But, she told me, there are also two female elephants, an Asian and an African, who "use their trunks to stimulate each other."

"Does that mean they're, like, girlfriends, or what?" I asked.

Ms. Campbell didn't know if the elephants could be considered girlfriends, but "same sex trunk stimulation," she informed me, "is well-known among elephants."

Well, I admit I was disappointed that the penguins turned out to be het. But lesbian elephant "fuck-buddies"?!...what a Gay Nineties concept.

Sentimental Journey

Today's my birthday and I'm feeling sorry for myself.

My lover and I have broken up. And on top of all that turmoil, I'm sitting here alone in my living room with my chin in my hand, surrounded by utter chaos.

I've found a new apartment, at least. But I've got to get out of this one by next week. All around me are dozens of half-packed corrugated cardboard boxes. Dozens more, that I've already filled up and sealed, are stacked seven feet high, leaning precariously, propped up against the walls.

On a normal day, I seem to spend half my time trying to track down where I've put my favorite pen. Amid all this upheaval, I can't even find my typewriter and my rolodex.

And now I am approaching some serious Moments of Truth: I have to make decisions about whether to take certain things along to the new place or throw them out.

This is extremely difficult for me, because I'm the kind of person who saves all sorts of things for purely sentimental reasons.

In fact, I hate to throw anything out. You never know when you might need that very thing—as it happens, I've sometimes discovered a potential use for the most useless-looking object not long after I've dumped it in the garbage.

And once something's hauled away in the dumpster—baby, it's gone forever.

But now that I'm moving, I'm determined to be toughminded about all this stuff I've been accumulating. I'm going to be ruthless in throwing away anything that is not absolutely essential. Ruthless, ruthless, ruthless.

121

My old electric fan, for example. It's broken and rusted—still I've resisted parting with it. But I can't lug a broken fan around with me wherever I move, just because it was there three lovers ago, humming along, a witness to some never-to-be-repeated steamy summer nights of lesbo longing consummated, of thrills fulfilled, back before the motor died. Can I?

Dump it. The motor died. That pretty much sums up that relationship, too.

Then there's my old mattress and box spring. Yes, a *bed* is essential—and a lot of memorable good times have taken place on this particular mattress. But now it's so soggy and soft that some of the springs have started popping out.

Dump it. Get a new bed, for heaven's sake! I do believe that hope springs eternal, but my bedsprings are on the verge of causing injury.

I think it's also time to say goodbye to this ancient livingroom sofa I'm sitting on. I bought it third-hand (or maybe fourth) at Betty's Resale Shop on Lincoln Avenue.

It was on this very sofa that I fell in love with one of my ex girlfriends. That in itself is enough to make me want to keep it. I remember the night we sat here drinking champagne, feeding each other grapes and cherries and licking whipped cream off each other, naked on the velveteen coverlet....

That was long before her dog "made a mistake" on one of the sofa pillows, and my dog "had an accident" on one of the legs.

And now, look at this, the stuffing is coming out in several places.

Dump it. Ashes to ashes, dust to dust, thrift shop to garbage truck.

So much for the debatable furniture.

I should also throw out all the useless little tokens of affection, the silly gifts, that ex lovers have given me on particular occasions through the years.

For instance, I've got a pile of items here in front of me on

122

the coffee table that I don't know what to do with:

A pair of windup chattering teeth. I got those as a joke gift from a lover who liked to keep the thermostat very low at her place, after I woke up shivering in her bed one cold winter night.

A battery operated raygun. From an ex who, like me, was into outer space movies at the time.

A purple teddy bear that says, "Bear With Me." What a bad week that was.

A windup plastic godzilla from the five-and-ten. It's covered with dust but sparks still fly out of its mouth when it walks.

A toy glockenspiel. I remember who gave it to me, but not the occasion.

Several small heart-shaped "I love you" balloons....

...And more.

All relics of bygone romances. But if I don't get serious about unloading this old stuff I have no use for, I may still have the plastic windup teeth when I don't have any real ones left in my mouth.

Papers are also a big problem. I seem constitutionally incapable of throwing out any scrap of paper that has something written on it—because then it's not just a piece of paper anymore, you know, it's a *document.* And if it has anything to do with lesbians (as many of my papers do), it's a *lesbian herstory document.*

I've already packed two dozen large file boxes full of them.

Let's see. What's this? A ticket stub from a romantic evening at the theatre, long ago. Is this *essential* to my current life? Of course not. Yet it just reminded me of that wonderful night when... she and I... (sigh)...

Here are another ex lover's telephone doodlings that I impulsively saved.

Essential? Dump 'em. After all, that one dumped you, didn't she?

Oh—here are some very graphic sexual letters from another ex. Now *that's* getting borderline essential. I never throw out letters....

At the rate I'm sorting through my things, I should be ready to move in a year or two.

Now honestly, I tell myself, isn't it time you let go of all this romantic flotsam and jetsam? Dump it all!

From the top of a tall, wobbly, haphazard stack of papers, a small card falls to the floor. I pick it up and recognize it immediately. It reads, "To My Honey—I'm thrilled that you are in the world—from Your Honey." It was once attached to a beautiful bouquet of tiger lilies I got for a past birthday.

It occurs to me suddenly that the day I got that card and bouquet was exactly seven years ago today.

I realize that I can't bring myself to part with any of these small love-tokens. I guess in some obscure way, these little reminders of sweet times are still meaningful and absolutely essential to my life, even now.

So does this mean that every time I move, I'll have to pack an additional two or three boxes of lesbian love memorabilia and junky little keepsakes? And haul them around with me for the rest of my life?

Yeah. I guess so.

If I'm lucky enough to keep getting them.

Strangers on a Train

I was in a pleasantly jiggling dining car on Amtrak, from Chicago to New York. I was on my way to visit my mother before heading up to Boston for Outwrite, the gay and lesbian writers' conference.

The attendant had seated me across from a handsome-looking, self-assured older woman who was also travelling alone.

The woman's steel-grey hair was cut very short. She wore an expensive white blouse, with lots of gold and diamond jewelry: several gold chain necklaces, and small diamond-stud earrings. On one hand she wore three gold rings, one of them with a vagina-shaped (to my way of thinking) onyx stone. I looked for overt lesbian signs—labrys, lambda, women's symbol—among the jewelry, but no, it was all standard commercial stuff.

I'm usually shy around strangers, but I needn't have worried about making small talk with this lady. As soon as the waitress took our orders, my dinner companion went into a long, nonstop monologue about herself that sounded as though it had been written for her by a publicity agent.

She was a widow who, some years ago, had had a terminal illness. She had been cured "by a miracle of the Lord." Ever since, she had been a woman preacher in the Pentecostal church.

I was a captive audience, as she went on and on, all through dinner, about her brilliant sermons and her calling from god. Although I'd barely said two words, she spoke to me as if she were certain that I was a sympathetic believer.

She had chutzpah, I'll grant her that.

Then she mentioned that she had just come back from a very successful "preaching tour" of Mexico, and was now planning a missionary trek to Africa to do god's work and "save the natives."

"Save the natives?" I sputtered, almost choking on my tasteless broccoli. I could feel my blood pressure going up.

Yes, she said—in fact, she had written an entire series of books to bring "the message of Our Lord" to all the poor suffering Third World people who of course need so desperately to hear it, to renounce their sins, so they can better their lives.

Oh boy. I'll bet, I thought to myself, that she also has a missionary "position" for all poor suffering lesbians and gays who desperately need to hear her "message" too, and renounce our so-called despicable ways.

But wait, I thought, perhaps I'm misjudging her, and she's more liberal than I'm giving her credit for.

Maybe she doesn't mean it quite the way it sounds.

Maybe I'm guilty of stereotyping here. Not all fundamentalists are racists and homophobes. Are they?

"My books have been very well-received," she said proudly. "Books are such an important way of spreading the word, you know."

Here was the first thing she'd said so far that I could relate to. I'm always on firm ground with book chat.

"Yes, well, as a matter of fact," I said, clearing my throat, "I don't know anything about the Pentecostal religion, but I've just begun reading a book about a man who grew up in a Pentecostal family in Texas."

This was true. It was a finalist in one of the categories for the Lambda Book Awards that year.

"Really?" she said, cocking her head with interest. "What book?"

"It's called *Strange Angel*, by Ben Davis. It's autobiographical. His ambition was to become a preacher. And then he discovered he was gay."

At the mere sound of "gay," her entire outgoing, folksy demeanor instantly changed. She gave me a stricken look and cringed.

Cringed.

The way I imagine Dracula might react if I had just taken out a small silver cross (speaking of religion) and quietly slipped it onto the tablecloth.

Hate was written all over the woman's face.

That pretty much confirmed where she stood on the gay issue.

"I've only read two chapters so far," I went on evenly, determined not to be intimidated, "so I don't know what happens, but I think he either left the church or got kicked out..."

"Oh, he got kicked out, you can bet on that."

She snorted.

I'm not exaggerating, she literally snorted, and then sneered, still assuming, so it appeared, that I was on her side. "He's probably that friend of Jim Bakker's from prison."

"Um, no," I said. "He's just a very religious gay man."

"You know," she said, spearing a rubbery carrot on her plate, "the company that published my second book went out of business. And the owner of that company, his son was gay."

She said this as if having a gay son was a curse that would automatically ensure any father's business collapse.

This is like a Hitchcock movie, I thought. This woman would be happy to see me and mine wiped off the face of the earth. I don't doubt that she would silence us in a second if she could, and in the name of goodness and charity. In fact, I wouldn't be surprised if she's a terminal closet case who has locked the closet door from the inside and swallowed the key. She even has that slick, self-assured, edgy manner of Robert Walker, the crazy guy in *Strangers on a Train*.

Well, I'm not Farley Granger, and I'm not going to let her assume that we're partners in crime.

"Now that I think of it," I said, "there's another book I'm

sure you'd find interesting: *Oranges Are Not the Only Fruit*, by Jeanette Winterson. About a girl growing up in a very religious family in the Pentecostal church in England."

Her hunched over, Dracula look had faded. "Oh? That's interesting."

"And as she grows up," I said, savoring my punch line, "she realizes she's a lesbian."

I smiled. Once again my dining companion suddenly looked afflicted and began making almost cartoonish snorting noises. Her behavior gave me new insight into the word "reactionary."

"Very good book," I assured her. "It's won a lot of literary prizes. They've even made it into a movie."

By this time it must have dawned on her.

"Well, here I've gone on and on about myself," she said. "What do you do for a living?"

"Me? I'm a writer," I said. "I work for a gay and lesbian newspaper in Chicago."

"Oh." She set her jaw, and her voice turned icy: "They have one of those there?"

"We have four," I chirped.

It was the first time I'd ever found an occasion to feel proud about the proliferation of publications spawned by Chicago's local gay newspaper wars. "Four."

She fidgeted with her teaspoon, and wouldn't look me in the eye. She seemed to have lost her energy.

Can it be, I thought, that she's actually afraid of me? And why? She's undoubtedly had dinner with gay men and lesbians before—she's just never *known* that they were.

"If you like, I'd be happy to write down the names of those books I mentioned," I said, ignoring the chill coming from her side of the table.

"Oh, thank you," she said, still polite but visibly uncomfortable. "But I have so many books already, I don't even have time to read the ones I've got."

She laughed nervously. Then she quickly paid for her dinner—charging it on her gold card, incidentally—and slunk back to her car.

To hatch some homophobic religious tract, probably.

I finished my coffee alone, as the train continued to jiggle along rhythmically toward New York, pleased at the thought that, at least, gay and lesbian literature has grown to such an extent that I knew not one but two widely available books on a topic as obscure to me as the Pentecostal gay and lesbian experience, books I could cull from my own reading experiences to contribute in a chance conversation with another "book lover."

There was a dusty old sign that used to hang in the reading room of my public library when I was a child: "Reading is Power."

So all you gay and lesbian writers out there, whoever you are, keep writing. Just the mention of two gay and lesbian books was enough to take the wind out of a homophobe's sails.

Remembering Audre

The last time I spoke with Audre Lorde was four years ago. I was doing a cover story on her for *Hot Wire* magazine. Audre was living on St. Croix, and Hurricane Gilbert had just passed through the islands. She had been without electricity for two days. We conducted our long distance phone interview with the expectation that at any moment we might be disconnected. But the line held, and we ended up talking for almost two hours.

Growing up Black in New York City, coming out as a young "gay girl" in Greenwich Village and Harlem, taking part in the feminist movement early on, and with her forthright personality and incisive intellect, Audre had plenty of subject matter for her poetry. But life gave her yet another topic, a burden she would rather not have assumed, but which she shared with us movingly in her writing: her fifteen-year battle against cancer.

First, a mastectomy in 1978. She wrote about her experience in *The Cancer Journals*, which won the 1981 Gay Book of the Year award:

"Living a self-conscious life, under the pressure of time, I work with the consciousness of death at my shoulder, not constantly, but often enough to leave a mark upon all of my life's decisions and actions. And it does not matter whether death comes next week or thirty years from now; this consciousness gives my life another breadth. It helps shape the words I speak, the ways I love, my political action, the strength of my vision and purpose, the depth of my appreciation of living."

I first met Audre when she came to Women and Children First Bookstore here in Chicago. Even though it was very crowded, I got the chance to talk with her for awhile—I had gone, years after her, to Hunter, the same all-girls' high school in New York that she did (she wrote about Hunter in *Zami*), and we both recalled our time there with fondness. I met her again in Montreal at the International Feminist Bookfair in 1988, where she seemed physically vigorous despite a continuing battle with liver cancer and surgery for ovarian cancer.

Audre traveled to Berlin several times a year for a special cancer treatment program. During our interview, she was optimistic. She talked at length about the interconnectedness of the political struggles of women, Blacks, and gays, and was involved in the women's movement in the West Indies.

In 1990 she was in Germany undergoing cancer treatment during the Lambda Book Awards ceremony (held in Las Vegas that year), and so could not receive the Publishing Triangle's Bill Whitehead Award in person. Jewelle Gomez read the fiery speech Audre had written for the occasion, in which she strongly advocated for the work of gay and lesbian writers of color.

I was hoping to see Audre again this summer at the Feminist Book Fair in Amsterdam, but by then she was gravely ill. The eminent Black South African writer Ellen Kuzwayo said she was on her way to visit Audre, to "say goodbye."

Audre always emphasized the importance of transforming our silences into language. In our interview, I asked her why it is often so difficult for people to say what we really feel and think.

"Because the stakes they offer us for being silent are so high," she answered. "The lie has always been that if we do not speak what we know to be true, then we will be allowed to take part in the fruits of whatever the imperfect systems are that we live in. But silence never bought us anything."

Silence doesn't make us happy, or safe, or beautiful, she said—it only makes our oppressors more comfortable.

"It is not the destiny of Black people to fulfill white America's mistakes. It's not the destiny of lesbians to fulfill the mistakes of the heterosexist world. It's not our destiny as women to relive male mistakes."

Audre stressed that when we open ourselves to each other's knowledge, and listen very carefully to the parts of each other's lives that we don't share, it makes us more powerful in fighting the battles we do share.

"The function of poetry is to make us more who we wish to be," she said.

Before her death two weeks ago, Audre Lorde—poet, essayist, and outspoken African-American lesbian feminist— had been named Poet Laureate of New York.

Farewell and blessings, Zami, Afrekete, Gamba Adisa.

Childhood's End

As an example of how we are all conditioned to heterosexuality from infancy, let's take a look at the classic children's feature film that generations have cooed over and found so magical and loveable, *Bambi*.

"I respect nature very much, and by watching and observing the habits of creatures of nature, man [sic] can learn a lot," Walt Disney said in 1942, at the time the feature-length cartoon was originally released.

The movie *Bambi* was based on a 1935 novel by Felix Salten about the life of a deer in the forest. Salten attempted to be realistic: the book portrayed predatory animals killing other animals as well as the dangers animals faced from predatory humans.

Yet despite Disney's pronouncements about learning a lot from nature, in *Bambi* he presents the opposite: human values—rigidly heteropatriarchal ones—imposed on animal behavior.

"Walt took out all the stuff from the book about survival of the fittest and animals killing each other," said Ollie Johnston, one of the supervising animators on the film.

Well, that sounds like a good idea, perhaps, to avoid frightening small children. But how did Disney change the way the animals related to each other?

"Good morning, Mrs. Quail," says a bunny in an apron.

"Good morning, Mrs. Rabbit."

When Thumper, Bambi's rabbit friend, is unruly, his mother scolds, "What did your father tell you this morning?"

This is Disney's idea of respecting nature and observing the habits of its creatures.

As a matter of fact, he depicts all the animal families with mothers watching over the children, and with fathers nowhere to be found.

I know a lot of kids who can certainly relate to that. But where *is* Mr. Quail, for instance? Perhaps he's busy at the office? The mysterious disappearance of all the daddy animals is never explained.

Sex roles are totally polarized along a heterosexual human model.

In the springtime, Thumper the rabbit falls in love. We see him lying in his girlfriend's lap. She strokes him with her long polished fingernails, bats her long eyelashes, and appears to have a human bosom.

Bambi falls in love with his fawnhood playmate Faline. Here Disney throws in all the stereotyped accoutrements: betrayal of male bonds, sleazy music, and stylized, cloying human seduction gestures.

It's really quite degenerate, watching animals act as whacked out as people.

Young Bambi has to fight another male for Faline in a dramatically animated scene with clashing red and yellow shadows. We are made to understand that Faline is in danger of being forced to go with the other buck if Bambi loses. Nobody in Disney's "natural" universe ever heard of an estrous cycle.

After Bambi "wins" Faline, she nudges and snuggles him, and they lie down together. Fade to a discreet G-rated morning after.

What happened, mommy? I understand that children like snuggly animals and furry pals that have some human qualities they can relate to. But does that mean that countless generations of cartoon bunnies and bears and squirrels and chipmunks and skunks and bluebirds have to be enlisted to reenact these simplistic, polarized sex roles and G-rated sex scenes over and over again?

Fifty years after *Bambi*, cartoons are still showing females with the floozoid music and long eyelashes, feigning weakness at the sight of an "eligible" male of the same species. I don't even see how heterosexuals can manage not to be outraged at the thought of their children watching this kind of true perversion of nature.

Bambi's father is the one father animal we get to see. He stands silhouetted high up on a ridge, aloof, omnipotent, like a god deigning to look down from heaven. "He's very brave and very wise," says Bambi's mother reverently. Bambi is suitably impressed. "He looked at me," he tells her, in a voice as childlike and anemic as Michael Jackson's.

Pathetic.

I think it's safe to say that more children have been traumatized through the years by the death of Bambi's mother than by any other scene in a Disney movie. I first saw the movie when I was about seven with my best friend, and she ran out of the theatre crying after Bambi's mother was shot by the horrible hunters.

Isn't it ironic that one of the few touches of genuine realism in *Bambi* has to be the murder of a female.

At the movie's end, we see Faline back in the glen where Bambi was born, with her own twin babies. History repeats itself, as the cliched cycle of nature is inculcated into the brains of more innocent children.

And again, daddy is not there. No child support in this forest. Instead, Bambi and his father both look down their long noses at the females from the high rocks. Bambi has now taken his place as an omnipotent, taciturn male, distant and unapproachable.

It isn't as if *Bambi* is the only movie in which this sort of stereotyping gets pushed on us, of course. The vast majority of movies, then and now, are heterosexual propaganda vehicles—including most cartoon films made specifically for very young audiences.

But the next time you coo over some supposedly innocuous cartoon, remember how Disney transformed an originally realistic story into his own anthropomorphic vision of sexuality and family life, making "nature" a paeon to patriarchy. Male supremacy, perfected in a heterosexual universe, is presented as not only unquestionable and eternal, but desirable. And so we are all led to think that heterosexual reality is ubiquitous and "eternal." And desirable.

What is really natural is what we do and are. Kicking off all the dreck we were bombarded with in childhood.

The wonder is that despite all our conditioning to act in these unnatural heterosexual patterns, our natural impulses toward our own sex emerge anyway.

Becoming a lesbian, being a lesbian. For me, that was growing up for real.

Dykelangelo

It's November, and here I am once again sitting at my workbench amid paint tubes, brushes, tweezers, needlenose pliers, glue gun, snippets of felt, tubs of plaster, rubber molds, and sculpey modelling clay. Doing my Art Thing. Making stuff for the 'Mountain Moving Coffeehouse Midwinter Minifest.'

The Minifest, usually held the first weekend in December, is a Chicago lesbian tradition that I really love—a day and evening of craft-browsing, noshing, and women-only socializing. More women come to the Minifest than any other coffeehouse event—so it's really an annual gathering of the community.

I display my handiwork to sell, but the real fun of being there is renewing acquaintances with women I may not have seen all year. I chat with old friends. I meet newly out lesbians, lesbians who have recently moved to the city, and lesbians from other parts of the Midwest who come to Chicago just for the Minifest. Some straight women I know come, too, to buy gifts for their friends.

Some people make batches of cookies this time of year; I make batches of lesbians. Lesbian refrigerator magnets, lesbian notecards, and, especially, lesbian tree ornaments. Some of the ornaments are purely symbolic: labryses, lambdas, triangles. Others are tiny detailed figurines I sculpt out of modelling compound: goddess images based on ancient female statuary, mythological images like mermaids (lesbian mermaids, of course). Some are simply women embracing or kissing. I make rubber molds of the original pieces I like best, so I can make duplicates of them cast in plaster.

This is all part of my ongoing artistic crusade to replace patriarchal imagery with lesbian iconography—a project that, I realize, may take several more lifetimes to complete.

My lesbian magnets, of course, are a bit more practical than the ornaments, since the refrigerator stays up all year. But it pleases the atheist in me to think of xmas trees loaded down with lesbian goddesses.

And never is the need for lesbian imagery more keenly felt than at xmas time.

Michelangelo believed that he didn't create his sculptures so much as he revealed them, by chipping away at the material surrounding each figure, releasing its soul, so to speak, from the stone block that previously encased it.

I feel the same way about my lesbian goddess ornaments. As I hack at my lump of clay, I can feel the soul of each tiny lesbian goddess being released from the surrounding super-sculpey modelling compound that previously encased it. As a lesbian atheist pagan, I have a tendency to lesbomorphize— that is, I believe lesbian spirits can be contained even in certain inanimate objects.

And I love sculpting naked women. I really get into it: forming their happy little faces, little arms draped lovingly around each other. But I confess that whenever I begin to shape their tiny crotches or their eensy breasts with almost microscopic nipples, I get a little squeamish. I don't want to injure them. I'm extra careful with my razor-sharp sculpting tool in these areas.

It almost seems like an invasion of their privacy.

I wonder if Michelangelo felt kinda funny sculpting David's fig leaf area....

"Now you've gone too far," an xmas-loving friend of mine scolded me, several years ago, when I showed her my latest work: it was simply a vulva with a hand groping toward it— nothing else. Painted gold.

"You expect people to hang *cunts* on their christmas trees?"

"Solstice trees," I corrected her.

"And is that supposed to be her own hand or someone else's?"

"It's Art," I said defensively. "So you tell me."

"It's *objectification*," she countered. "Naked lesbians and big breasted goddesses are one thing, but this is sheer body parts."

"It's not objectification, it's the opposite—it's *lesbomorphism*," I said. "Think: how would a lesbian sex organ act if it were alive all by itself? Would it hop up and down, and instinctively nuzzle against you?"

I guess I was imagining something along the lines of The *Nutcracker Suite*, with dancing vulvas instead of sugar plum fairies.

But my friend was unmoved. "It might just pee everywhere," she said.

"No way!" I said. "If it didn't have a brain, it wouldn't have a bladder either."

At the Minifest that year, one of the first women to come up to my table looked over my rows of hanging ornaments, and her eyes zeroed right in on one of the tiny golden vulvas.

She pinched up her face and squinted. She grabbed it off the rack, and held it in her hands.

Uh-oh, I thought, here comes a lecture on my crude insensitivity, on objectifying women, maybe even accusations of pornography.

"What is this?" she said, puzzled, staring intently at the tiny crotch in her palm. "A tree?"

Now I grant you, my artistry could probably stand some improvement. But I've learned that lesbian spirit, like beauty itself, is often in the eye of the beholder.

"Passing" and the Price of Silence

The biographical dictionary *Notable American Women* has two listings under the name "Harper." Both of them were Black women.

The first, Frances Watkins Harper, was born in Baltimore in 1825. She was an antislavery lecturer, a poet, and a writer—in fact, she wrote the first short story by an African-American ever to be published.

The other woman listed is lda Husted Harper, born in Indiana in 1851. She was a journalist and a staunch feminist who had a "long and fruitful association" with Susan B. Anthony. She co-wrote, with Anthony, the *History of Woman Suffrage*. Harper lived with Anthony, and travelled with her on lecture tours and convention trips in the United States and abroad. Harper also wrote Anthony's three-volume biography.

I know of another African-American woman named Harper who is of historical significance as well: Minnie Buckingham Harper of West Virginia became the first Black woman to be a legislator in the United States, when she joined the West Virginia House of Representatives in 1928.

She was my grandmother.

Minnie Harper might have made a career for herself in politics despite the political handicaps of being Black and female. But she had a "secret" that political opponents could capitalize on: she had an illegitimate child. In 1928, no woman with political aspirations could overcome that stigma.

Have things changed all that much in the last 60 years?

Minnie's illegitimate son—her only child—was my father.

She married Ebenezer Harper, a prominent Black politician of the time. My father was raised in a large, extended "colored" family in a proudly African-American cultural environment; Minnie had 11 sisters and brothers, and her husband had 12.

My father graduated from an all-Black segregated high school. When he went off to college, however, he began hiding his background, "passing for white." For over 30 years he kept the secret of his family and his race, even (or should I say especially) from his white wife, my mother. As I was growing up, in New York City, I was told that my father's mother was dead.

In fact, Minnie lived to be 95.

What did "passing" cost my father in self-esteem? I can recall him many times sitting through dinner conversations with my mother's relatives as they made vicious, stupid anti-Black jokes and comments. He chuckled at the racist jokes of neighbors. He covered his tracks by agreeing with them, by making racist remarks himself.

When I began working in the Civil Rights movement in the Sixties—ignorant of the fact I had a whole side of my family that was African-American—my father would argue with me, saying my Black friends were a bad influence on me.

My father's secret "came out" only after Minnie died and relatives on his side of the family began calling—and inadvertently got my mother on the phone.

Oops.

The following months were very exciting and interesting ones for me—among other things, I got to meet my older half-sister, who I hadn't known existed. My father had been married to an African-American woman before he married my mother—something else he had neglected to mention.

I know, I know, it sounds like a soap opera. It even felt like I was in the middle of one, for a while. My mother engaged in a whole lot of damage control, so her side of the family wouldn't find out, and so the neighbors wouldn't know.

It still burns me up to think that I was never given the

chance to meet my history-making grandmother. I have no doubt that there are millions of other people in this country whose African-American ancestry has been kept from them.

Yet even long after my mother had made peace with my father for lying to her all those years, getting information out of my father was like the proverbial pulling of teeth. Once I had bits and pieces of the story, I found old documents in libraries, and I confronted him with them. If I pressed him with questions, he would reluctantly shed light on another small part of the puzzle of his history.

I think it had been so long since he had been honest that lying had become second nature for him.

Yet when my father died, he left behind a thousand-page typewritten manuscript, an autobiographical novel, in which he described what it was like to be a 'colored' child who looked white. He described the wonderful people he knew before he severed himself from his upbringing. In this manuscript, he firmly denounced the evils of slavery and discrimination.

Sadly, these were things he never said out loud while he was alive.

I often think about my father when I hear someone make a homophobic remark. Those of us who are gay or lesbian who can "pass for straight" in this world have to constantly make choices—about how far we are prepared to confront homophobes, how we are going to handle it when someone makes an anti-gay or lesbian joke or comment in our presence, how "visible" we are going to be in a world that assumes everyone is straight unless they "divulge" that they are not.

One of the reasons I work for gay and lesbian rights is that I couldn't live the way my father did—by hiding, covering your tracks, and, worst of all, imitating the very people who are putting you down, and thus putting down your own brothers and sisters. In fact, if you think you are "blending in," you are deceiving yourself and destroying your own integrity. Every slur you let go by unchallenged is a painful reminder of your complicity. I saw it happen to my father.

Sexism, racism, and homophobia are, for me, linked in

more than theory—I can see how they have directly affected my life and the lives of my relatives for at least three generations. Thinking of my grandmother and father, I can't help but think of all the "spinster" aunts and "bachelor" uncles who have vanished from families around the country, and all the families that have been split apart by "secrets"—when people are measured against a standard not of their own making, outside of their own worth. And we all lose something when these connections are lost.

It is so easy for silence to close over history. The straight white men who control almost all of the media, real estate, and business interests have always felt justified in defining their reality as the norm. They don't even see how deeply their own programming goes—that the standards they call "universal" are no such thing.

We must not allow imposed definitions of who we are, any of us, to influence and confine us any more. Otherwise the powers that be will say, as they are more than happy to, that those of us who are not rich, straight, white, or male don't really matter in the scheme of things.

Nothing could be further from the truth.

We must encourage each other to give voice to our real selves, our real experiences, and to our many and complex realities. Our integrity, if not our survival, depends upon it.

Bermuda Pink Triangle

I'm leafing through a book called *The World's Last Mysteries.* It has most of the same kind of stuff you see in similar books about Great Unsolved Questions: Was there a lost continent of Atlantis, where was it, and what happened to it? Why did the Nazca people draw huge pictures on the flat plains of Peru that could only be seen from high in the sky? Did a black hole hit Siberia?

Some of these questions are genuinely intriguing. Other such questions, it seems to me, just display a Western bias: the assumption that nobody but Westerners have ever figured out how to do anything impressive. Who carved the giant stone statues on Easter Island? Take a guess: the Easter Islanders! Who built the pyramids in Egypt? Could it have been Egyptians? Could the great stone temples of the Maya have actually been built (gasp!) by Mayans?

Never mind, too, that the really mysterious things going on in the universe—like what IS it, anyway?—are nowhere near as easily answered as who built what here on Earth.

This particular book—published by the Reader's Digest and chock-full of interesting photos and "artists' conceptions" of ancient cities and so forth—is a cut above similar-themed ones, but still the language is rather sensationalistic. About the huge, mysterious explosion in Siberia that occurred in 1908, for example, it says:

"Was it a giant meteorite? An atomic blast from a crippled alien spaceship? Or was it a collision with the most chilling rogue body in the universe—an object so dense that it twists the very laws of time and space? Did, in fact, a black hole hit Siberia?"

Television shows, too, often delve into these Mysteries, always previewing them with a lot of fanfare and spooky music. Unravelling the secrets of Stonehenge. Investigating the disappearances in the Bermuda Triangle. And so on.

I used to love watching and reading about this kind of stuff, actually. But lately I've been getting more and more frustrated: I have leafed through every page of this particular book, and others like it, and watched dozens of TV shows that purport to explore the Greatest Mysteries in the World, and I have yet to see the slightest mention of the Greatest Mystery of all.

That is, the mystery of how the world can be full of gay people and yet nobody sees them.

I'm willing to believe that the lost continent of Atlantis lies sunk under the Bermuda Triangle. Fine. It makes sense to me that people vanish through an invisible triangle and get sunk. Why not? I see it every day. People appear briefly and then disappear—into straight jobs, for example—and are never heard of again. Or sometimes resurface periodically, after holiday visits to their relatives. It happens to people all the time, so why not to whole ships and planes?

Is it a giant meteorite that keeps men and women in Egypt and Peru and Siberia and even Salisbury Plain from living a real and honest life as gay men and lesbians? No. As dramatic and sensationalistic as it seems, the fact is that *a giant cloud of homophobia encircles the world*—and *that's* the "most chilling rogue body in the universe." It's so dense that it can "twist the very laws of time and space," and of the truth of our existence.

It's homophobia that sinks us and explodes us into oblivion and makes black holes out of our lives. When do we get to see that Mystery on television?

Until the question of the gay men and lesbians who have been erased from human history is fully investigated, and until the question of all the lesbians and gay men around the world who are made invisible by fear, hatred, and ignorance is addressed, I'm not going to take any of these other so-called Mysteries seriously anymore.

As far as I'm concerned, Stonehenge was built by ancient pagan lesbians as a giant calculator to chart the course of the sun goddess through the sky.

The silent stone sentinels on Easter Island were built by Easter Island lesbians to protest the enforced silence of lesbians everywhere.

The black hole in Siberia was created by Siberian lesbians to protest the fact that while our existence isn't even acknowledged, we simultaneously get blamed and blasted for being who we are.

The Egyptian pyramids were built by Egyptian lesbians of fantastically advanced mathematical and architectural ability. The Mayan pyramids were built by Mayan lesbians as a wonder for all the world to see.

Lesbians undoubtedly built the fabulous advanced culture of Atlantis, too, and it was sunk by jealous barbaric straight people.

So there.

As lesbians, we have been and are still all lost in the Bermuda Triangle, and will be as long as lesbian and gay existence on this planet is simultaneously made invisible and persecuted.

Until that changes, I declare the other Great Mysteries solved: Lesbians of all ages and all cultures are responsible for them.

This is the only advantage of being invisible: *How do they know we aren't?*

146

Duck Soup

Times are certainly changing. These days, if I have any doubt about whether or not some celebrity is queer, my mother can often tell me. She's a seventy-one-year-old widow who watches Oprah, Sally Jessy, and Donahue, listens to Rush Limbaugh, and reads all the tabloids.

"Hillary Clinton is a lesbian," she announced on the phone last week.

Theoretically, I believe that all women, deep down, are really lesbians. I'm a lesbomaniac, and prone to wishful thinking. But when my mother fingered the First Lady, so to speak, I admit I felt some skepticism.

"Oh, Ma," I said. "How do you know that?"

"Well, if she isn't, how come she hangs out with them?"

"With who?"

"With all those other lesbians. Like that Donna Shalala— now, I *know* she's a lesbian, because my next-door-neighbor's sister worked for her once, and says she never had a boy-friend. And Shalala was very close with that one in the New York State legislature, I forget her name, it begins with a B— she's a lesbian, too. And that one who smokes a pipe...."

"But Ma," I protested, laughing, "Even if a lot of her friends are lesbians, that still doesn't mean Hillary is. Maybe she hangs out with them because they're all intelligent, honest, reliable, extraordinary, fantastic women."

"Oh I'm not knocking them, believe me. I got nothing against them. I say, who cares if they are?"

"So you're saying that if it walks like a duck and talks like a duck...?"

"Yeah. It's a duck. And get this: Hillary and Clinton don't sleep together."

"How on earth do you know that?"

"I read it in the paper this morning. So here's Hillary, she don't even sleep with him but he's hiring all her friends. Why? Because Clinton has to do what his wife says now. Because she covered for him before, see?"

"Huh?"

"Look," my mother said. "Think a minute. Clinton was sleeping with that Jennifer Flowers woman for eleven years. Eleven years! She had all these documents to prove it."

"Well, I don't know about that, but so what if he was?"

"Don't you see? There's no way Hillary couldn't have known that Clinton was fooling around."

"Yeah, if he was...So?"

"So, if she's a lesbian, she wouldn't care if he had a girl-friend."

I can't believe I'm having this conversation with my mother. "Ma, there must be millions of straight women whose husbands are fooling around with someone else...."

"But it didn't *bother* her."

"How do you know it didn't bother her?"

"Because she let it go on all that time," she said.

"What could she have done about it? What about that mistress Bush was supposed to have had all those years...?"

"Yeah, that's true, he did. I heard about that too."

"So does that mean Barbara Bush is a lesbian?"

"No! Barbara's not a lesbian. But Hillary is. Wait and see. And that girlfriend of Bush's, well, I can understand her position: a woman thrown in with a bunch of men like that, naturally you're going to start up with one of them."

"Not me," I reminded her.

"Well, not me either," she said. "The ladies at the Seniors say to me, 'Why don't you go out with some nice man?' and I tell them, 'I wouldn't want the best man there is—I don't care if he shit gold.' That always shocks them."

"But, Ma, maybe then they'll think *you're* a lesbian...."

"I don't care if they do," my mother said. "By now, everybody's got one in the family."

We both had to laugh at that.

For members of the lesbian literati, bibliophiles. and anyone who might be curious as to approximately when particular events referred to in the columns took place:

Most of the Lesbomania columns in this book first appeared in *Outlines* and *Nightlines* in Chicago—some in slightly different form, and a few with different titles. Some of them later appeared in *The Weekly News* (Miami), the *Washington Blade* (DC), *Bay Windows* (Boston), and *HOT WIRE: The Journal of Women's Music and Culture* (Chicago). "Elizabethan Drama"and "Michiguilt" are also included in the collection *Lesbian Culture: An Anthology*, edited by Julia Penelope and Susan Wolfe. "Quest for the Ancient Lesbonauts," "Dykes Along the Nile," and several other columns have been performed in slide-show versions as well.

Dates of first publication:

Alone at Last, *Nightlines* September 18, 1991.
Bad Attitude, *Nightlines* April 24, 1991.
Back to Nature, *Nightlines* August 22, 1990.
Beyond the Fringe, *Nightlines* May 8, 1991.
Presto-Change-O!, *Nightlines* September 12, 1990.
Fest Side Story, *Nightlines* March 18, 1992.
Bermuda Pink Triangle, *Outlines* January Issue 1994.
The Face On Mars Comes Out, *Outlines* Pride Issue July 1992.
Femmes Penetrate Butch Stronghold, *Nightlines* April 25, 1992.
Fighting Erupts Between Butches and Femmes, *Nightlines* April 15 1992.
Gertie, You're So Wordy, *Nightlines* January 29, 1992.
The Ghost of Christmas Past, *Nightlines* December 23, 1992.
Give Me an L!, *Nightlines* July 24, 1991.
Godzilla Emerges From Closet, Nightlines May 16, 1990.
Heart to Heart, *Nightlines* November 25, 1992.
High Visibility, *Nightlines* February 26, 1992.
Highway 61 Revisited, *Nightlines* July 18, 1990.
I'm Okay, You're Okay, *Nightlines* July 10, 1991.
A House is Not A Homo, *Nightlines* April 25, 1990.
I'm a Maniac, Maniac, *Nightlines*, July 24 1991.
Kissing Cousins, *Nightlines* August 8, 1990.
Michiguilt, *Nightlines* August 15, 1990.
Negotiations Open at Beaver Dam, *Nightlines* May 13, 1992.
New Under the Sun, *Outlines* Pride Issue July 1991.
No Place Like Home, *Nightlines* 21, 1991.
On Passing and the Price of Silence, *Outlines* February 1990.
Practice Makes Perfect, *Nightlines* February 17, 1993.
Quest for the Ancient Lesbonauts, *Nightlines* August 7, 1991.
Read My Lips, *Nightlines* July 31, 1991.
Remembering Audre, *Nightlines* December 2, 1992.
Sentimental Journey, *Nightlines* September 11, 1991.
Shangri-La-La, *Nightlines* August 14, 1991.
Space Invaders, *Nightlines* September 5, 1990.
Strangers on a Train, *Nightlines* March 10, 1993.
Tension Mounts at Beaver Dam, *Nightlines* April Fool's Day 1992.
Through the Looking Glass, *Nightlines* September 26, 1990.
The Valentine Grinch, *Nightlines* February 12, 1992.
What Becomes A Legend Most, *Nightlines* July 4, 1990.
When Things of the Spirit Come First, *Nightlines* March 24, 1993.
Zoo Story, *Nightlines* March 4, 1992.